TRUMP'S TAX CUT GUIDE

Understanding the New Tax Changes for Tax Years 2018, 2019 and Beyond

Michael Rutherford

consult a licensed professional before attempting any techniques outlined in this book.

By reading this document, the reader agrees that under no circumstances is the author responsible for any losses, direct or indirect, which are incurred as a result of the use of information contained within this document, including, but not limited to, — errors, omissions, or inaccuracies.

Table of Contents

Introduction

The Tax Cuts and Jobs Act

On December 22, 2017, extensive tax legislation after the Tax Reform Act of 1986 was enacted. The Tax Cuts and Jobs Act (TCJA), passed in 2017, represents the Republican Party's plan for tax reform. While the impact of the law on employers is not what was initially proposed, the effort to digest and internalize the changes will, nonetheless, be substantial, particularly as it has severe implications throughout the United States.

As with any comprehensive legislation, there are certain portions that will require more answers and clarifications from IRS regulations. We should also expect impending technical revisions to address inadvertent errors or unforeseen consequences. Given the levels of uncertainty, the process for analyzing the TCJA and coordinating regulations across various IRS agencies could stretch well into 2019 and beyond. In the meantime, I encourage individuals and businesses to take on an active role and seek clarification on provisions which they think may affect them, acting prudently in the absence of IRS guidance.

This book seeks to provide a comprehensive layout of the TCJA's provisions, detailing the list of changes as well as analyzing how these changes may affect both individuals and businesses. By reading this book, you will be able to understand how the workings behind taxation and all the other intricacies that may seem insignificant could actually play a huge role in the amount of taxes that you have to pay. The book has been structured in such a manner whereby it first talks about taxation pertaining to individuals before dwelling into taxes regarding corporations. Finally, it will focus on taxation laws governing some of the other more specific areas such as farming businesses.

Chapter **1**

Understanding Your Taxes

Importance of Knowing Your Laws

Every year, usually around April, you will be required to report your income to the Internal Revenue Service (IRS) through a series of documentation and forms. For the average worker, tax money is withheld from paychecks throughout the year. During the filing of income, the employer will report to the IRS the amount paid to each worker while the worker will report to the IRS his or her income and expenses. The IRS, then, compares these numbers to ensure that each pays the correct amount of taxes. If the amount of money withheld from the worker's paycheck throughout the year is insufficient to cover the amount of taxes the worker has to pay, he or she will then have to pay back the difference from his or her pocket. On the contrary, if the amount of money withheld is more than the amount of taxes that the worker is required to pay, he or she will be refunded with a check from the government, reflecting the difference.

Taxes are an inevitable process of growing up and a sign of adulthood. As long as you are a citizen of any current country in the world today, you will be required to pay taxes. Taxes constitute one of the primary sources of revenue for the government of any country. These taxes are what help fund social security programs, public amenities, infrastructure, and the defense of your country. Therefore, paying taxes can be considered a form of civic duty, and people have been paying them, although it is uncertain whether this will be the case if paying taxes is not a requirement of law. Admit it, no one likes paying taxes. Given a choice, we would all prefer keeping all of our salaries to ourselves. Nevertheless, there are multiple concessions implemented by the government which may reduce the amount of taxes that one has to pay. Unfortunately, various laws are governing these concessions which make it difficult for the layman to optimize these concessions to their benefits. However, for an individual who is well-versed in the various provisions, he or she will then be able to take full advantage of these concessions to minimize the amount of payable taxes.

As mentioned earlier in the introduction, the TCJA has resulted in an overhaul of previous tax laws. Such amendments include restructuring the individual income tax brackets and the corresponding tax rates; suspending the usage of personal exemptions; restricting itemized deductions; a 21% flat tax rate for businesses and corporations; amendments to Section 168 & 179; and many more. This book seeks to provide a comprehensive review of all these various changes and how these changes can affect all of you. So, pay attention to every single chapter because an oversight to these rules may end up costing you more than you should be paying.

Federal Income Tax and Brackets

New Income Brackets and Tax Rates

The TCJA maintains seven income tax brackets even though President Trump initially wanted three income tax brackets. The income brackets are as follows. Do note that these amendments will expire by 2025.

For unmarried individuals, the following table presents the revamped income brackets and their corresponding tax rates. In general, personal tax rates have fallen.

Income Brackets	Tax Rates
≤ $9,525	10%
$9526 - $38,700	12%
$38,701 - $82,500	22%
$82,501 - $157,500	24%
$157,501 - $200,000	32%
$200,001 - $500,000	35%
≥ $500,001	37%

Table 1: Unmarried Individuals other than surviving spouses and Heads of Households

For the head of households, the following table presents the revamped income brackets and their corresponding tax rates. For example, if your taxable income for the year of 2018 is $50,000, you will be required to pay $1,360, plus 12% of the excess of $13,600 which equates to $1,360 plus $4,368 resulting in a total of $5,728.

Income Brackets	Tax Rates
≤ $13,600	10%
$13,601 - $51,800	12%
$51,801 - $82,500	22%
$82,501 - $157,500	24%
$157,500 - $200,000	32%
$200,001 - $500,000	35%
≥ $500,001	37%

Table 2: Head of Households

For married individuals who are filing joint returns and surviving spouses, the following table presents the revamped income brackets and their corresponding tax rates. For example, a married couple has a taxable income of $80,000. They are required to pay a combined tax of $8,907 plus 22% of the excess over $77,400 which equate to $8,907 plus $572 resulting in a total of $9479.

Income Brackets	Tax Rates
≤ $19,050	10%
$19,501 - $77,400	12%
$77,400 - $165,000	22%
$165,501 - $315,000	24%
$315,001 - $400,000	32%
$400,001 - $600,000	35%

≥ $600,001	37%

Table 3: Married Individuals filing joint returns and surviving spouses

For married individuals filing separate returns, the following table presents the revamped income brackets and their corresponding tax rates.

Income Brackets	Tax Rates
≤ $9,525	10%
$9526 - $38,700	12%
$38,701 - $82,500	22%
$82,501 - $157,500	24%
$157,501 - $200,000	32%
$200,001 - $300,000	35%
≥ $300,001	37%

Table 4: Married Individuals filing separate returns

Federal Income tax withholding, supplemental wages, and backup tax

Pre-TCJA era

Before the TCJA, employers were required to withhold federal income tax from the wages that they paid to their employees using the tables and methods provided by the IRS and Form W-4 provided by the employees. For each taxation year, the IRS revises Publication 15 which contains the income tax withholding tables and percentages based on the inflation adjustments to the individual tax brackets and the corresponding allowances and exemption. The IRS also publishes the updated Publication 15, for each tax year reflecting the appropriate inflation adjustments. Individuals should refer to the Publication 15 as a guide when filing for taxes.

Assuming that salary charge was retained from the customary wages of the representative in the present or going before expense year and supplemental wages are independently recognized and don't surpass $1 million, businesses may alternatively utilize a level rate of pay charge retaining on supplemental wages. This is tied to the third tax bracket, which for 2017 was 25%. If the employee's year-to-date supplemental wages surpass $1 million, it is compulsory for employers to withhold at the highest rate bracket, which for 2017 was 39.6%.

Organizations are, likewise, required to retain reinforcement charge from non-wage installments under specific conditions (e.g., when payees neglect to give their citizen distinguishing proof number). The retaining reinforcement rate is fixed to the fourth duty section, which for 2017 was 28%.

Individual income tax withholding and Form W-4 instructions apply toU.S.nonresident aliens. Publication 15 contains the instructions for income tax withholding on wages paid toU.S.non-resident employees.

As will be mentioned in Chapter 2, the individual income tax rates have changed. Also, the personal exemption deduction is also suspended. Notwithstanding, the law states that the IRS may oversee the paid charge retaining rules under IRC without respect to this arrangement for duty years starting before January 1, 2019. Whether the pay maintaining rules according to the personal exemption remain unchanged for 2018 is at the discretion of the Treasury and the IRS.

On January 11, 2018, the IRS distributed Notice 1036 which contains the much anticipated 2018 percentage method tables for income tax withholding incorporating the changes as a result of the TCJA. Employers were tasked to roll out the new withholding methods immediately, before February 16, 2018. Employers were directed to use the 2017 withholding tables and methods until the new tables are officially published.

For an employee whose year-to-date supplemental wages exceed $1 million, employers have to withhold their wages at the highest rate bracket of 37%. Employers may also use a flat income tax withholding rate of 22% (down from 25% in 2017) on supplemental wages of up to $1 million. However, this option is only available if the income tax was withheld from regular wages in the current or the previous year and the supplemental wages were separately identified. Officially, the TCJA called for a rate of 28%; however, the IRS has overruled it and stated that it would refer to the third tax bracket for this rate, as it has done in prior years.

The alternative withholding rate is tied to the fourth tax bracket of 24%.

The IRS has disseminated the amounts that were included in the wages of nonresident aliens to compute federal income tax withholding. The IRS will need to update IRS Note 1392 to show the amendments with the effects TCJA (e.g., shelving of personal allowances for years 2018 through 2025).

The IRS clarifies that it has planned the salary charge retaining tables to work with the representative's present Form W-4. This way, even though the derivation for individual remittances and ordered findings subject to the 2% floor are suspended for duty years 2018 through 2025, the 2018 pay charge retaining tables keep on accommodating individual allowance with values higher than they were in 2017. The IRS states that there is no mandatory requirement at this time that all employees furnish a new Form W-4.

Employees are required to begin using the 2018 Form W-4 on and after March 30, 2018. For the tax year 2018, the IRS warns that some employees with more complex tax situations could face the possibility of being under-withheld. For example, employees who itemize their deductions, coupled with various occupations or people with more than one employment in a year are urged to survey their assessment circumstances and decide whether a change through their Form W-4 is essential. The IRS suggests specialists, especially those with more than one salary in their family unit, to check their 2018 retention.

Changes in Inflation

Traditionally, the Consumer Price Index (CPI) is used as the primary formula in measuring the increase or decrease in the cost of living in the US. The premise of this calculation is based on the fact that a dollar fifty years ago does not equate to the same purchasing power of a dollar today. However, under the TCJA, the CPI will be replaced by a slightly different index, the Chained Consumer Price Index (Chained CPI) in determining the annual inflation rate.

The critical difference between the two indexes is that the CPI only factors in the changes in pricing of a particular product whereas the Chained CPI factors in other possible substitutes that consumers can make in response to the increment of prices in that product. For example, if a Bosc pear increases in price, the CPI will reflect that increment accordingly. However, the Chained CPI will look at other possible substitutions that consumers purchase, such as the Williams pear.

The differing considerations and calculations between the two indexes in determining inflation rates will probably result in slower increments for the Chained CPI as compared to the CPI. In correspondence, social security benefits will then increase much slower as well as compared to using the CPI because of the inclusion of possible cheaper or similarly-priced substitutions when the cost of a product increases. With regard to taxation, the usage of the Chained CPI then slows down the rate of increment for the income brackets. This decrease in the rate of increment of tax thresholds could potentially result in more taxpayers getting forced into higher brackets at a faster pace, and by extension, having to pay higher taxes. Of course, this is assuming that the income of the people increases in conjunction with the increase in inflation as well.

A crucial point that one should take note of is the switch from using the CPI to the Chained CPI will be adopted permanently unlike several other aspects of the TCJA, which expire by 2025.

Chapter **2**

Tax Breaks (1)

Above-the-line Deductions

Above-the-line deductions are subtracted from one's income to determine your adjusted gross income (AGI). The higher the deduction, the lower one's taxable income. The AGI affects one's qualification for some tax cuts and can trigger specific duties. The TCJA rolls out some noteworthy improvements to two above-the-line deductions. Whether an individual applies for standard deduction or itemized deduction, he or she will still be eligible for above-the-line-deductions.

Moving Expenses

Section 132 allows an exclusion from wages for reasons for moving expenses. What this means is that you become eligible to receive a deduction on your tax returns due to the expenses incurred in moving. However, becomes applicable in cases where you move from one place to another for work purposes. The expenses are refunded or paid by the employer condition to the fact that those moving expenses

12

are deductible under Section 217. Under Section 217, the deduction applies for the expenses of moving personal and household items from place of old residency to the new location, the first 30 days of storage for a domestic move, and housing and travel expenses accrued during the travel time from the place of former residency to the new residence. Special rules apply to international moves. Non-taxable moving expense reimbursements paid directly to employees are reported on Form W-2, box 12, code P.

Repayments for moving costs made to workers or paid straightforwardly to outsiders on and after January 1, 2018, through December 31, 2025, will be incorporated into wages. A particular case to this arrangement applies to individuals from the Armed Forces on active obligation moving according to a military request an episode to a lasting difference in station.

Except for moving costs identified with Armed Forces individuals on dynamic obligation, bosses should change their duty setup settings for profit to mirror the incorporation in wages from January 1, 2018. Detailing in Form W-2, box 12, code P won't have any significant bearing except for the Armed Forces where non-assessable moving cost installments still apply. A comparing change is, likewise, required for state and nearby pay expense and retaining purposes for those states that adjust to the IRC as of January 1, 2018.

Settlements – sexual harassment

Under Section 162, businesses are allowed a deduction for the amount paid with regard to legal settlements following employee complaints such as discrimination and sexual harassment.

With the effect of the sums paid or brought about after December 22, 2017, and under the new Section 162(q), no business derivation takes into account settlements or lawyer charges identified with such settlements paid compliant with lewd behavior or sexual maltreatment if the installment is dependent upon a nondisclosure understanding. Note that there is no adjustment in the government finance charge treatment of worker settlement grants. So, what are some of the steps that businesses can take?

- **Approach contemplations.** In light of the reasoning restriction for lewd behavior grants, businesses ought to consider the degree to which grant beneficiaries will be required to go into a nondisclosure understanding.

- **General ledger accounts.** It will be imperative that businesses have a general record account or other systems for distinguishing non-deductible settlement grants.

Alimony Payments

A divorce agreement finalized after December 31, 2019, will not qualify for alimony deductions from a taxpayers' taxable income for 2019. For the individual receiving the alimony, the amount received as alimony will not be considered as part of the taxable income. This means that the recipient of the alimony would have a lower amount of tax to pay as compared to the individual paying the alimony, provided that all else remains equal. However, these amendments will only take effect on the taxable income for 2019 and will remain permanent. In other words, for the year of 2018, the old policy still applies. The payer can still deduct the amount of alimony paid from his or her taxable income while the recipient will have to include the amount received in his or her taxable income. However, not all above-the-line deductions were eliminated. Those that remain include:

- Self-employed health insurance. Self-employed personnel can continue to deduct health insurance premiums from their total income capped to the amount of the profits from the business.

- Health Savings Account contributions. Individuals who continuously make monetary contributions to their Health Savings Account can deduct this amount from their total income.

- Retirement Plan contributions by self-employed taxpayers. Self-employed personnel who make annual contributions to their retirement plans such as solo 401 (k) plans can deduct these amounts from their total income as well.

- IRA Contributions. Constant contributions to IRA accounts (depending on one's annual threshold limits) may be deductible.

- 50% of self-employment taxes. Self-employed personnel can deduct half of the 12.4% Social Security Tax on net self-employment income, up to an annual ceiling. A 2.9% Medicare tax on all net self-employment income is also deductible.

- Penalty on early savings withdrawals. Individuals who withdrew their savings early from saving accounts from banks are required to pay a specific penalty to the bank. Such penalties are deductible.

- Student loan interest. For individuals whose AGI is below a ceiling amount, up to $2,500 of student loan interest is deductible.

- Tuition and fees. Taxpayers who are paying tuition fees for themselves or other people are eligible to deduct up to $14,000. However, the taxpayer must not have claimed the American Opportunity Tax Credit or Lifetime Learning Credit.

It is essential to review your above-the-line deductions because they affect your Adjusted Gross Income (AGI). Your AGI is crucial because it determines whether you are eligible for further tax breaks or concessions. Not done correctly, it can trigger certain additional taxes that you would have to pay, and I am sure that you do not want that. Once you have calculated your AGI, the next step is to determine what sort of deductions are you eligible for or which deductions helps you to retain the most cash. There are two main deductions which one can opt for.

Taxpayers can determine which deduction they are more suited for. For itemized deductions, a variety of costs and contributions can be reduced from their taxable income. These include student loan interests, medical costs, or even charitable contributions. Usually, the taxpayer will only opt for itemized deductions if it surmounts to more than the standard deduction, based on their filing status. To claim these deductions, the individuals need to produce some form of evidence to prove the authenticity of those items that the individual wishes to be considered for deduction. Not everyone will itemize deductions simply because of the hassle required in sieving out proofs and shreds of evidence for every single item. Furthermore, there have been several amendments to limit and abolish many itemized deductions, and they have also increased the incentive for taxpayers to opt for standard deductions. Thus, it is essential for the taxpayers to relook at their filing for the year 2018.

Tax breaks are concessions given by the government that help to reduce the amount of one's taxable income, which translates into a lower payable tax. This helps to ease the financial burden of individuals, especially those from lower-income families and those who have multiple dependents at home.

There are mainly two types of tax breaks. First, personal exemptions whereby a certain amount is subtracted from an individual's taxable income based on the profile of the individual. Second, deductions are calculated based on the expenses of a particular individual. Both personal exemptions and deductions are tax breaks that help to reduce one's taxable income and ultimately the amount of payable taxes. With the implementation of the TCJA, there have been several drastic changes to the benefits of personal exemptions and deductions. Hence, it is paramount to know the difference between the two to optimize the benefits of these tax breaks while filing for taxation.

Personal Exemptions

Personal exemption itself is a relatively simple concept – you subtract a predetermined amount of cash for each qualified individual from your family unit when registering assessable pay. They are determined based on the number of dependents that an individual has. Before the implementation of the TCJA, taxpayers were able to claim a personal exemption of $4,050 each for themselves, their spouses, or any dependents. However, you are only allowed to claim an exemption for yourself if no one else names you as a dependent when submitting their tax return. Also, an individual can only be considered as a dependent provided that the individual receives minimum financial support of 50% from you. The implementation of the TCJA has abolished personal exemptions with effect since the beginning of 2018. Therefore, individuals who have been relying on personal exemptions as a source of tax breaks need to relook when filing for their taxes for the year 2018 so as to not end up owing money to the IRS.

Chapter 3

Tax Breaks (2)

Itemized Deductions

Before the implementation of the TCJA, many taxpayers have been relying on itemized deductions to reduce their payable taxes. Therefore, if you happen to be one of them, you might want to pay more attention to this particular chapter as I will be listing the several amendments to itemized deductions that will kick in with the TCJA. After which, I will come out with an analysis of these amendments, and you can decide for yourself if itemized deductions will be able to optimize your tax breaks. The following items listed below are those that have been affected by the TCJA:

State and Local Tax Deductions (SALT)

State and local taxes refer to items like state taxes, local income, sales taxes, personal property taxes, etc. The initial proposal in the TCJA meant to scrap all state and local deductions. While it had survived, the deductions have taken a massive knock to it. Starting in 2018 and going through

2025, taxpayers can only claim a total deduction of no more than $10,000 for all the state and local taxes combined. Taxpayers who have been living in high tax states, such as California, will see a considerable reduction of their State and Local Tax deduction and hence itemizing it does not make much sense. Of course, the effects of the capping of this deduction differs according to the situation. Taxpayers are encouraged to recalculate the total amount of state and local taxes that they are required to pay to adjust accordingly to this new policy.

Mortgage Interest Deduction

Mortgage interest refers to the interest incurred from a loan taken to purchase a property. Under the TCJA, mortgage interests continue to be eligible for deduction. However, there are two critical amendments to it. First, only the interest of the first $750,000 of mortgage debt is deductible for mortgages incurred after December 14, 2017. This may not necessarily affect taxpayers whose houses are worth below the limit of $750,000. However, in locations where property prices tend to skyrocket, such as that in New York City, this cap of $750,000 may pose a huge problem for taxpayers living there. Second, interest on home equity loans will only be deductible if the loan is being used to improve the current home. Loans for any other purposes will no longer be qualified for deduction even if the loan was incurred before December 15, 2017.

Charitable Contribution Deduction

In a bid to encourage more public donations, the TCJA

raised the limit on charitable contribution deductions from 50% of adjusted gross income to 60%. Do note that these charitable acts have to be based on altruistic reasons rather than personal gains. For example, there have been incidents whereby charitable acts were made to colleges in exchange for priority seating during college athletic events. While such acts do not contravene the existing law, payments made for such reasons will not be applicable for deductions.

Medical Expense Deduction

The TCJA has amended the policy revolving around medical expense deduction as well. Previously, any unreimbursed medical expenses which exceeded 10% of the taxpayers' adjusted gross income could be deducted. Under the TCJA, this percentage has been lowered to 7.5%. This means that more medical expenses can be deducted. Note that the date of implementation for the medical expense deduction has been rolled back to January 1, 2017.

Miscellaneous Itemized subtractions as a result of the 2% floor

Tax preparation fees expenses and non-refunded employee business expenses deductions are some of the deductions that are suspended for 2018-2025. This suspension includes the home-office deduction affecting mainly freelancers and employees who have been working from home.

Personal Casualty Deduction

Commencing 2018 until 2025, personal casualties will no longer be applicable for the Personal Casualty Deduction, unless the casualty was a result of a disaster and was officially pronounced as such by the President of the United States.

Suspending the reduction of itemized deductions

Before The Tax Cuts and Jobs Act of 2-17 was established, if your AGI exceeded the allowable limit, specific deductions were lowered by 3% of the AGI sum over the limit (this should not exceed 80% of allowed deductions). For 2018-2025, the reduction has been placed in an inactive status.

For taxpayers who have been reliant on itemizing deductions, it may not be financially sound to rely on it anymore, given the new policy implementations under the TCJA — for example, assuming that an individual who files as a single person in 2017 prior to the TCJA had total itemized deductions of $8,500, or $2,150 more $6,350, the previous standard deduction rate. Assume that this individual had the same total itemized deduction of $8,500 again in 2018. Instead of having a $2,150 more in deductible expenses as compared to using the standard deduction, the taxpayers would lose out, since the new standard deduction is at $12,000. Therefore, by using the standard deduction, the taxpayer can deduct $3,500 more than itemizing. It is of paramount importance for individuals who have been itemizing their deductions to relook and recalculate their filings for the year of 2018 to optimize the benefits encompassed in the TCJA.

Standard Deduction

The standard deduction is a tax break whereby the individuals can automatically deduct from their adjusted gross income a fixed sum of money. If the standard deduction that you qualify for is higher than the total sum of itemized deductions you qualify for, then the standard deduction becomes the obvious choice. The TCJA has also, on average, doubled the standard deduction rates. Table 5 lists the current amount of standard deductions that individuals from each category are applicable for. These amounts will be indexed for inflation subsequently from 2019 onwards. The amount of standard deduction that one qualifies depends on a few factors: your age, your income, and your filing status.

Filing Status	Age	Standard Deduction
Single or married filing separately	Under 65	$12,000
	65 or older	$13,600
Married and filing jointly	Under 65 (both spouses)	$24,000
	65 or older (one spouse)	$25,300
	65 or older (both spouses)	$26,600
Head of Household	Under 65	$18,000
	65 or older	$19,600
Qualifying widow(er)	Under 65	$24,000
	65 or older	$25,300

Table 5: Standard Deductions Requirements

For people who are unsure of the deductions that you are

eligible for, you can always rely on the IRS tool which is designed to help one determine how much can be deducted from his or her income in less than five minutes.

Nevertheless, do note that there are specific scenarios whereby one will not be eligible for any standard deduction, and so, it is essential to make sure that you do not fall into any of this categories when filing for taxes:

- Filing a tax return throughout less than 12 months to amend one's yearly accounting period.

- A non-resident alien at any point during the tax year.

- Married but filing separately and your spouse options for itemized deductions.

- Estates, partnerships, collective trust funds, and trusts are also not eligible for the standard deduction.

The question to ask is whether the increased amount of standard deductions is able to offset the repeal of personal exemptions. Unfortunately, the answer to this question will vary across individuals. For some, the increased amount of standard deductions may somewhat smoothen the effects of the repealing of personal exemptions. However, for people with multiple dependents or who are used to itemizing deductions, these new changes that came along with the TCJA might result in higher due taxes– of course, these families can and should leverage on the multiple benefits from certain family tax credits to reduce their payable taxes.

Essentially, the TCJA has created multiple restrictions on several itemized deductions. Therefore, individuals who have traditionally relied on itemizing should review their existing itemized deductions under the TCJA, and compare it to the total number of allowed tax deductions. With the TCJA's twofold increase of the typical deduction for 2018 and reduction of the overall benefits attained by itemized deduction, many employers and the general public who have itemized may find themselves no longer gaining any advantage from itemizing.

Chapter 4

Family-Based Concessions

A family-based tax law

Many provisions in the TCJA have been favorable towards the traditional family such as the new income tax structures for married couples and the elimination of alimony deduction from taxable income for the receiving spouse. Nevertheless, the provision that highlights the importance of family is that of the child tax and other dependents' credits. Unlike the previous provisions, the tax breaks given to children and other dependents are in the form of credits. In the eyes of many individuals, tax credits are perceived as highly valuable, and they are right to think so. Tax credits directly reduce an individual's tax bill rather than reducing one's adjusted gross income. In other words, tax credits directly reduce the outstanding amount of taxes that one has to pay. Raising a child is a costly affair and is set to be even so in the future. One of the reasons for decreasing childbirth rates all over the world is the increasing cost of having a child. Thus, the increased benefits given to families with children underscore the importance of families in American society.

Child Tax Credits

Before the implementation of the TCJA, individuals above the age of 18 were not eligible for a tax credit. Commencing in the tax year of 2018, with the effects of the TCJA kicking in, the number of child credits that an individual is eligible for will be doubled to $2,000 per child of 17 and below. If the credits exceed the taxes owed, these credits up to an amount of $1,400 per child will be refunded. Do note that the earned income threshold for the refundable credit is lowered to $2,500. This means that lower-income families will have more support from the government in terms of lowered taxes and refunds.

However, the Child Tax Credits are not subject to inflation meaning that the tax credits will be capped at $2,000. The only component that is subjected to inflation is the refunded amount of credit for families with children under the age of 17. Aforementioned, it is currently capped at $1,400. This amount will gradually increase with inflation until it hits the full value of the Child Tax Credit of $2,000. The phase-out for the Child Tax Credit has been increased to $400,000 for joint filers and $200,000 for other filers. This means that anyone is eligible for the Child Tax Credit regardless of income provided that your taxable income does not surpass the phase-out levels.

Other Dependents Credits

Why was this created?

Before the TCJA, the tax credits were only eligible for children under the age of 17. However, in reality, we all know that families do not only consist of children. There could also be other dependents in the family such as one's parents or other relatives, whatever the reason may be. Furthermore, there has been an increasing number of children above the age of 17 who continue living with their parents, even as they have already started college. This puts the financial burden on their parents. Hence, the TCJA makes tax credit available to more family members or other dependents as compared to the past. Under the new law, families with other dependents – including children aged 17-18 and even full-time college students aged 19-24 are eligible for a non-refundable credit of up to $500 each. The credits for these other dependents will only begin to phase out when the adjusted gross income exceeds $400,000 for joint filers and $200,000 for all other filers.

There are, however, several criteria for an individual to be qualified as a dependent. The dependent must be related to the taxpayer in one or several ways (grandchild, daughter, etc.). The dependent does not have to live with the taxpayer throughout the year. However, an important condition to note is that the dependent but must have resided in the taxpayer's household or place of home more than 6 months. There are certain exemptions to this clause of course, such as parents of the taxpayer. The dependent must have also received more than half of his or her financial support from the taxpayer throughout the tax year. The dependent must be a U.S. citizen or resident, such as a green card holder. Non-citizen residents of Canada and Mexico do not qualify. These conditions are a mirror of the Child Tax Credit. In this case, the exception is that it is not mandatory for the dependent to possess a valid Social Security number. Any tax identification number will suffice provided that the dependent meets all the other criteria. A point to note is that the taxpayer cannot claim the credit for his or her spouse if they are married and are filing a joint return. Neither can the taxpayer claim for him or herself. There are no restrictions whatsoever against taxpayers claiming this credit if they are filing separate returns even though they are married.

These provisions under the new Child Tax Credit and Other Dependents Credits will all expire after 2025 which is in line with the law and all previous administration with regard to taxation laws. Hence, even if the income thresholds will not be indexed for inflation, meaning that the credit will lose its value over time, there should not be that huge of a financial impact on families from now until 2025 since increments in inflation will probably be much slower with the usage of the chained CPI formula.

Chapter 5

Other Forms of Taxes

This chapter focuses on the various types of uncommon taxes that one may be liable for but is unaware of. Some of these taxes include the Alternative Minimum Tax (AMT), the 'Kiddie' Tax, and the Estate Gift Tax. For the AMT, it tends to apply mainly to high-income earners. The 'Kiddie' Tax is a tax created for children below the age of 17 mainly to discourage adults from transferring their assets to their children so as to reduce the amount of payable income tax. The Estate Gift Tax is applicable mainly to adults who possess high valued assets or high amounts of cash who are thinking of giving these things away to another individual. If you think any of these taxes may apply to you, then do pay attention to this chapter.

Alternative Minimum Tax (AMT)

What is the AMT?

As the name suggests, the AMT is a unique form of tax system. It does not have any standard deductions or personal exemptions. Is does not allow itemized deductions from sources such as state and local income taxes. For example, if your AGI is over 7.5 percent, only then you may find that you are eligible for the deduction of medical expenses. Hence, the AMT is much higher than that of the regular tax. Not only is AMT ineligible for tax breaks, but it also recalculates income tax after taking into consideration the individual's adjusted gross income and bringing specific tax preference inclusions. Tax unique items are income-generating items that are usually tax-free. Examples of such items include interest on private activity municipal bonds, the qualifying exclusion for small business stock, and surplus nonmaterial drilling expenditure for the oil and gas entities if the amount exceeds 40% of the AMT income. The AMT exemption is then subtracted to determine the final taxable figure. With the implementation of the TCJA, the AMT exemption figure is $70,300 for individual filers. For married joint filers, the AMT exemption amount figure is $109,400. The resulting payable taxes are then calculated from the final taxable income (after AMT exemption) based on the relevant rate schedule.

There are only two tax rates: 26% and 28%. The tax rate is 26% for income below the AMT threshold and 28% for those above it. In 2018, it was capped at $191,500 for single taxpayers and those who are married filing jointly. It is $97,750 for married filing separately. The AMT exemption figure is much higher than the standard amount exemption. However, it starts to disappear after you reach a certain income level called the phase-out level. Once your income hits the phase-out level, $0.25 of the exemption disappears for every dollar above the phase-out level.

Am I liable for it?

A taxpayer that earns more than the AMT exemption figure ($70,300 for individual filers and $109,400 for married joint filers) and uses the deductions must calculate his or her taxes two times – the first calculation for the regular income tax and the second calculation for the AMT. Individuals must then pay the higher of both taxes calculated. It is important to note that taxpayers with an alternative minimum tax income (AMTI) over a certain threshold do not qualify for the AMT exemption. For 2018-2025, the thresholds are $500,000 for individuals and $1 million for those who are married and filing jointly.

The AMT was created to prevent wealthy taxpayers from escaping their fair share of tax liability through breaks. Thus, it can be seen as progressive tax legislation since it focuses on the rich. However, this portion of the TCJA was not indexed to inflation or tax cuts. This can cause bracket creep, a condition whereby the upper-middle-income taxpayers are subjected to paying the AMT instead of the wealthy taxpayers for whom the AMT was created for. In 2015, however, Congress passed a law indexing the AMT exemption amount to inflation. These amounts will be annually adjusted for inflation until the provision expires after 2025. Nevertheless, with the introduction of the chained CPI in determining inflation rates rather than the CPI, bracket creep could still possibly occur.

The TCJA has the capacity to lower the number of taxpayers for a short duration. These are taxpayers who have been mandated to pay the AMT. This is performed by raising the AMT exemption sum and the phase-out limits of the AMT exemptions. However, the AMT is more likely to snare married taxpayers with children for several reasons. First, they often have higher incomes, especially if both parents are working. Second, the AMT does not have additional exemptions for each household member. Third, there is no 'marriage bonus' under the AMT.

These AMT amendments are valid only until 2025, after which the exemption reverts to pre-Tax Act levels in 2026.

Kiddie Tax

The Kiddie Tax is a name given to a special tax law created in 1986 dealing with investment and free income tax for individuals under 17 years of age. Before 2018, the IRS taxed any income exceeding the predetermined threshold at the rate of the child's guardian. With the TCJA, when the child's income exceeds the threshold, the Kiddie Tax kicks in and applies a taxation structure where the amount earned dictates the tax rate, unlike the previous reliance on the tax rate of the child's parents. Only a small portion of the child's unearned income is taxed at the parents' marginal rate (if higher).

One popular and shrewd tax strategy has always been for parents to transfer investments or other income-producing assets to members of the family that fall under lower income tax brackets to ensure the full utilization of the low income tax rates provided to them. The Kiddie Tax and its implementation impedes the carrying out of such advantages so that individuals pay their fair share of taxes. The Kiddie Tax is applicable usually to students aged ranging from 19-23 and also children who are below 18.

The TCJA revamped the clauses in the Kiddie Tax and clamps down harder on individuals who attempt to transfer their assets to their children. With the revamped Kiddie Tax, the tax on a child's unearned income is determined by rates for estates and trust, and the tax brackets. It is currently fixed at 37% for taxable income up to $12,500. For married couples filing together, the 37% rate will not kick in unless the total joint income reaches $600,000. What this means is that taxation levied on the children's unearned income will have higher percentages than their parents' earnings. The table below illustrates the different rates for a child's unearned income.

Brackets of Unearned Income	Tax Rate
≤ $2,500	10%
$2,551 - $9,150	24%
$9,151 - $12,500	35%
≥ $12,501	37%

Table 6: Kiddie Tax Rates

Estate Gift Tax

Christmas day is one of the most celebrated occasions in America when people shower each other with gifts, with hopeful kids wishing for a present from Santa Claus. However, do you know that a gift can be taxed, and this tax will be paid for by the donor? In other words, even Santa Claus is liable to pay his taxes and seeing the number of presents that he delivers in a year, I would think that he has high taxes to pay. He is introducing the U.S. Federal Gift Tax!

The U.S. Federal Gift Tax is imposed on cash and properties that individuals give to others. It is paid for by the donor, not the beneficiary of the gift, even though the IRS has been known to claim taxes from the beneficiary when the donor fails to pay. The rationale underlying the implementation of this tax is to prevent individuals from giving away their money and property while they are alive to avoid having to pay an estate tax when they die. There are certain exemptions and exclusions, of course, that taxpayers can use to reduce and even eliminate this tax liability.

The IRS comprehends a gift as something you give for which you do not receive full considerations in return. Something can fall under the definition of a gift if the beneficiary of your generosity does not give you something of equal fair market value or money. Based on this provision, it appears that Christmas gifts are, indeed, taxable!

I am just kidding! Not all gifts are taxable! There are specific requirements that a gift needs to fulfill before it qualifies as being taxable. A U.S. citizen can give up to $152,000 in cash or property to a spouse who is not a U.S. citizen. This limit is subjected to inflation, which means that you can expect the limit to increase marginally yearly. The unlimited marital deduction also allows a U.S. citizen to give his or her spouse as much as he or she likes without paying a gift tax. One can also give unlimited funds for education or healthcare as long as you pay the institutions directly. In other words, you cannot give the money to the beneficiaries directly such that the beneficiary pays the providers or school directly. You are also allowed to give gifts to qualified charitable organizations and some political organizations without incurring the gift tax as well.

Annual Gift Tax Exclusion

The annual gift tax exclusion is a sum of money you are allowed to give away per person, per year, tax-free. Gifts given either as a lump sum amount or given in portions to the same person over a period of one year are not taxed if the total amount does not surpass $15,000 as of 2019. The annual gift tax exclusion is calculated individually, depending on each gift recipient. In other words, you can give $15,000 in cash to one of your sons, a $15,000 car to another son in the same year, and a $15,000 bag to your daughter and none of it requires you to pay tax. Every donor is entitled to this $15,000 exclusion. Therefore, married couples have a total of $30,000 limit.

The lifetime gift tax exemption comprises of the total amount one can give away tax-free over their whole lifetime. It is an aggregate amount rather than by person or by year, and it is in addition to the annual exclusion. For example, if you gave your daughter $30,000 cash at once, $15,000 of that would fall under the annual exclusion, and the lifetime exemption would, by extension, cover the remaining $15,000. The American Taxpayer Act of 2013 (ATRA) indexed the lifetime exemptions for inflation, so it increases year by year. However, it is shared with the U.S. Federal Estate Tax, so your lifetime blessings decrease the measure of exception you have left to later shield your bequest from tax collection on the off chance that you apply it to your lifetime endowments over the prohibition sum. For example, if you give $150,000 cash to your son in 2019, $135,000 of that amount becomes taxable after subtracting the $15,000 annual exclusion. You can either choose to pay your gift taxes in that same year, or you can deduct the total remaining amount of $135,000 from your lifetime exemption. For the latter, the $135,000 taxable amount reduces your 2019 lifetime exemption from $11.4 million to $11,265,000. The marginal tax rate for all taxes remains at 40%.

The TCJA spiked the exemption up to $11.8 million in 2018, effectively doubling it from the year before. It was adjusted to $11.4 million in 2019 to keep pace with inflation. These adjustments, however, are mere temporal as the TCJA expires at the end of 2025 unless Congress chooses to renew the legislation. Otherwise, the exemptions would fall back to the $5 million range.

One thing the TCJA does not do is to repeal the federal gift and estate tax, as initially proposed. However, the TCJA does in the meantime attempt to minimize the potential impact of such gift related taxes.

While there is a pretty low probability that one will be liable of federal estate tax liability, it does not encourage that families simply ignore estate planning. Within a family, there are many nontax issues to consider, such as asset protection, guardianship of minor children and family business succession. In addition, it is uncertain how states will react to the TCJA, especially for states with a strong historical enforcement of state estate taxes.

It is also imperative to make a mental note that the exemptions are scheduled to revert to their previous levels in

2026, and there is no guarantee that a future Congress would not further lower the exemption amounts that one is eligible for. However, it would be shrewd to exploit the existing high exemptions when filing for taxes.

While the TCJA shields significantly more citizens from these duties, those with estates in the range of $6 million to $11 million territories still need to consider potential post-2025 estate tax liability in their estate planning. Even though their bequests would escape estate taxes, if they were to pass on while the second exemption is in effect, they could face such expenses if they live past 2025. Any citizen who could be liable to pay gift and estate taxes after 2025 might want to consider making endowments currently to exploit the higher exclusions while they are still accessible.

It is crucial to factor taxes into your estate planning especially if you live in a state with an established estate tax. Even before the TCJA, many states had already imposed estate taxes even though at a lower threshold than the federal government. With the TCJA, the differences will be even more pronounced.

Finally, income tax planning, which rose to prominence in estate planning when exemptions increased to $5 million years ago, will be playing an even more significant part of estate planning. For example, continual possession of assets until death may be advantageous if estate taxes are not of any concern. However, the recipient will be subjected to capital gains tax when he or she eventually receives the appreciated asset and sells it in the market. When an appreciated asset is inherited, on the other hand, the recipient's basis is "stepped up" to the asset's market value on the date of death, erasing the built-in capital gain. So, retaining appreciating assets until death can save significant income tax.

Chapter 6

Retirement Accounts

Traditional IRAs

A traditional individual retirement account (IRA) offers tax advantages to savers and allowing one to invest in the future. The key features of a traditional IRA are as follows:

- Contributions made to the IRA can be deducted from their taxable income.

- Gains made within the IRA account through investments will not be taxed until they are being withdrawn.

- Retirement distributions will be taxed as ordinary income once withdrawn.

- Without meeting specific criteria, early withdrawals may be taxed as income and a 10% penalty may be imposed as well.

Due to the upfront tax deduction, traditional IRAs are especially attractive if you perceive your future tax rates when you are retired to be significantly lower than your current tax rates. This is especially so for individuals during their peak earning years and who are employed in a high-paying job.

Everyone is rightfully eligible to apply for a traditional IRA. However, not everyone gets to deduct their contributions made to their respective IRA. The eligibility for doing so depends on whether the individual or his or her spouse is covered by an employer retirement plan, like a 401(k), and income. An individual or his or her spouse with a retirement plan at work will automatically have his or her deductions reduced, then eliminated once a certain threshold is reached. Contributions can be made, but they will not be tax-deductible. The rates are as follows:

Filing Status	Full Deduction	Partial Deduction	No Deduction
Married but Filing jointly and a retirement plan at work that covers you.	2018: ≤ $101,000 2019: ≤ $103,000	2018: $101,001 - $120,999 2019: $103,001 - $122,999	2018: ≥ $121,000 2019: ≥ $123,000
Married filing jointly and a retirement plan at work that covers your spouse.	2018: ≤ $189,000 2019: ≤ $193,000	2018: $189,001 - $198,999 2019: $193,001 - $202,999	2018: ≥ $199,000 2019: ≥ $203,000
A retirement plan at work that covers married filing separate and you or your spouse.	2018: Not Available 2019: Not Available	2018: < $10,000 2019: < $10,000	2018: ≥ $10,000 2019: ≥ $10,000
Single or head of household	2018: ≤ $63,000 2019: ≤ $64,000	2018: $63,001 - $72999 2019: $64,001 - $73,999	2018: ≥ $73,000 2019: ≥ $74,000

Table 7: Rates for Traditional IRA

Roth IRAs

The Roth IRA is a form of retirement account that is embedded with valuable tax benefits, such as tax-free growth on your investments. The eligibility for a Roth IRA account is dependent on your income. Contrary to a traditional IRA, contributions made to a Roth IRA are not tax-deductible. The upside to this is that the investment earnings in the Roth IRA account are tax-free even when these earnings are being withdrawn in retirement. Retirement withdrawals from a traditional IRA account will be deemed as income and taxed accordingly. The key features of a Roth IRA are as follows:

- The account is not subjected to the required minimum distributions required from a traditional IRA or 401(k) beginning at age 70.5. Money accumulated within the Roth IRA can be handed down as an inheritance.

- As the contributions to a Roth IRA have been taxed upfront during the initial phase of contribution, withdrawing this amount at a later point in time will not result in these withdrawals being taxed again.

- Upon reaching the age of 59.5 and holding the account for five years, you can receive distributions, including earnings, from a Roth IRA without paying federal taxes.

- One is allowed to use money within the Roth IRA to pay for qualified college expenses without an early distribution penalty. However, do note that only the penalty is waived. Early usage of earnings is still subjected to income taxes.

A Roth conversion refers to the transferring of all or parts of the remaining amount in an existing traditional IRA into a Roth IRA. The greatest difference between the traditional IRA and a Roth IRA lies in how and when one's money is taxed. The traditional IRA operates in a way such that your contributions are tax-deductible in the year that these contributions were made. The Roth IRA operates in a way that your withdrawals in retirement are not taxed. Whether a traditional IRA or a Roth IRA is more beneficial to you depends on you. The rates are as follows:

Filing Status	Modified AGI	Maximum Contribution
Married filing jointly or qualifying widow(er)	2018: < $189,000 2019: < $193,000	2018: $5,500 ($6,500 if 50 or older) 2019: $6,000 ($7,000 if 50 or older)
	2018: $189,000 to $198,999 2019: $193,000 to $202,999	Contribution is reduced
	2018: ≥ $199,000 2019: ≥ $203,000	Not eligible
Single, head of household or married filing separately (if you did not live with spouse during year)	2018: < $120,000 2019: < $122,000	2018: $5,500 ($6,500 if 50 or older) 2019: $6,000 ($7,000 if 50 or older)
	2018: $120,000 to $134,999 2019: $122,000 to $136,999	Contribution is reduced
	2018: ≥ $135,000 2019: ≥ $137,000	Not eligible
Married filing separately (if you lived with spouse at any time during the year)	2018: < $10,000 2019: < $10,000	Contribution is reduced
	2018: ≥ $10,000 2019: ≥ $10,000	Not eligible

Table 8: Roth IRA rates

If you perceive your tax rate to be higher in retirement, meaning you will be earning a higher income, choose a Roth IRA and its delayed tax benefit. If you expect lower rates in retirement, meaning you will be earning a lower income, choose a traditional IRA and its upfront tax advantage.

Roth Conversions

The quickest way to deposit a significant sum of money into a Roth IRA is to take your traditional IRA and then turn it into a Roth IRA. The conversion will be treated as a taxable distribution from your traditional IRA because you are being treated to have received a payout from the traditional account with the money before depositing this amount into the new Roth account. However, by doing so, you will incur a bigger federal income tax bill for this year, if this conversion is done before year-end. The tax rates are based on the Federal Income Tax Rate Brackets.

Low current tax cost for converting plus gaining an indemnity against higher tax rates on your income in future years will accumulate in your Roth account and create a fertile ground for the Roth conversion strategy. First, direct your contributions into a traditional IRA, which has unlimited income threshold. Then, transfer the money into a Roth IRA using a Roth conversion. However, make sure that you understand the tax consequences before using this strategy.

The TCJA has adequately disposed of one's capacity to

reverse a Roth change. Since 1998, people have been empowered to convert either all or part of their traditional IRA to a Roth IRA, at the expense of paying the necessary taxes based on the converted amount. There have been loads of changes throughout the years since 1998; for the conversion from Traditional IRA to Roth IRA in some years, the taxable income on conversion could be spread over the years. Preceding 2010, just people with modified adjusted gross income under $100,000 were allowed to change over; presently, there is no pay impediment. For a few years, only traditional IRAs could be converted over to Roth IRAs; presently, a distribution from practically any customary retirement plan can be exchanged (changed over) to a Roth IRA. At one time, Roth IRAs were the only conceivable goal for conversion contributions.

Over the 20-year period of the existence of Roth IRAs, the person who chooses to convert to a Roth IRA has had a unique privilege: the option to change his or her mind and reverse the conversion, until the extended due date of his or her tax return for the conversion year, also called "recharacterization."However, a contribution to one IRA can still be recharacterized as a contribution to another IRA, unless as stated otherwise or limited by the statute or by the IRS.

Chapter 7

Affordable Care Act (Obamacare)

The Affordable Care Act (ACA), more popularly known as Obamacare, was signed into law by President Obama on March 23, 2010. The reason why I think this particular provision deserves a chapter on its own is precisely because of controversies involved when trying to get the law passed and also the extent of the impact that it has over all Americans. The ACA has three primary goals:

- To allow more people to gain access to affordable health insurance. Under the law, consumers now receive what is known as "premium tax credits," or commonly called subsidies. These reduce the costs for households with earnings that typically fall between the 100% and 400% range of the federal poverty level.

- One of its aims is to allow the Medicaid program to reach out and cover all adults with earnings that fall lower than the federal poverty level's 138% poverty rate. (Not all states have expanded their Medicaid programs).

- It supports innovative medical care delivery methods designed to lower the costs of health care generally.

Individual Mandate

The ACA created a requirement for people to have health insurance that satisfies certain standards, also known as the minimum essential coverage. This requirement is also known as the "individual mandate." Before the effects of the TCJA kicked in, an individual who does not have health insurance or one that meets the standards as written in the ACA, will have to pay a fine when filing for taxes in the subsequent year. Premium tax credits are available to individuals below certain income thresholds who do not have access to employer-provided or government coverage and who purchase their coverage through a state or federal exchange (also referred to as "marketplace" coverage).

Individuals purchase medical coverage for assurance against the hazard that they may become ill or harmed. When you sign on to a protection plan, your hazard gets shared by every other person in the arrangement. In a specific year, a few people get restorative treatment worth more than the premiums they paid, while others don't get as much as what they paid. Alternatively, then again as such, a few people get increasingly out of their protection plan, since they require progressively restorative consideration, and consequently cost the insurance agency more cash.

For the insurance agency to have enough cash to pay for its clients' cases, there must be more individuals on the arrangement who are solid than there are individuals who are unfortunate. On the off chance that everybody on the arrangement had real diseases or wounds and kept running up enormous doctor's visit expenses, the insurance agency probably won't have enough cash to pay every one of the cases.

The discussion emerges because individuals who are wiped out are bound to need to purchase protection than individuals who are youthful and moderately stable. Before the ACA, insurance agencies tackled this issue by screening candidates and declining to safeguard individuals who were bound to have costly medical issues since they had previous conditions.

The ACA mandated that insurance companies must accept everyone who applied, even those with pre-existing conditions. The ACA attempted to make it this way so organizations could never again prevent individuals' inclusion because of securing antecedent conditions. That implied the insurance agencies could never again screen out undesirable individuals who were probably going to cost them a ton of cash.

The underlying issue of people only wanting health insurance when they are sick results in more people with high medical bills and less relatively healthy people paying premiums but making fewer claims. To offset this imbalance, insurance companies would tend to increase their premiums such that they can meet the medical payouts of their clients. However, such a strategy is unsustainable and will serve to raise medical costs in the U.S. The individual mandate was, therefore, a solution designed to balance out this imbalance. By enforcing that everyone enrolls in a health insurance plan with minimum essential coverage – through the imposing of a tax penalty - the ACA will be able to introduce a number of healthy people into the health insurance system. The goal is to ensure that health insurances protect more people and also a decrease in premium rates due to an increase in insurance subscribers.

TCJA – A Republican Victory

The Republicans have been opposing the ACA almost immediately since its introduction by then President Obama in 2003. During the campaign of current President Trump, he swore to abolish the ACA within his first 100 days of office. True enough, one of his immediate tasks upon taking office in 2016 was to repeal the ACA. Fortunately, or unfortunately, his attempt failed not once but twice. While the Democrats were celebrating their victory, President Trump managed to find a way to negate the effects of the ACA without actually repealing it.

Among the many provisions in the TCJA enacted by Congress is one that effectively abolishes the effects of the individual health insurance mandate under the ACA. Subject to certain exemptions, the individual mandate requires all Americans to obtain minimally adequate health insurance for themselves and their dependents. Those that fail to do so are required to pay a tax penalty to the IRS. The TCJA has abolished this penalty, and so, individuals who now fail to obtain health insurance will have to pay nothing. This will make obtaining health insurance a purely voluntary decision for individuals as it was before Obamacare was enacted. This change could become permanent.

Republicans had two primary reasons for removing the effect of the individual mandate penalty. First, by doing so, it allows the Republicans to fulfill their campaign promises in repealing at least portions of the ACA. Second, repealing the individual mandate would free up government spending which is needed to cushion their proposed tax cuts successfully. Do note that according to the law, it is still compulsory for most individuals to be covered under approved health insurance; the TCJA merely removes the tax penalty for individuals who fail to comply. Furthermore, the individual mandate is still in effect for the 2017 and 2018 tax years, and those who fail to comply will still be subjected to the ACA's steep penalty. Two important conclusions can be drawn from here. First, the Marketplace and the premium tax credits from the ACA are still available if you qualify. Second, employers with more than 50 full-time equivalent employees are still required to offer affordable minimum essential coverage and meet reporting requirements. Failure to comply will result in the employer getting penalized following the ACA.

According to the Congressional Budget Office (CBO)'s November 2017 report, repealing the individual mandate would decrease deficits by around $338 million from 2018 to 2027. The projected savings from the repeal of the individual mandate are the result of a projected 4 million Americans losing insurance by 2019. CBO predicts that by 2027, 5 million individuals will lose their nongroup market coverage, 5 million will lose Medicaid coverage, and 3 million will lose employer-sponsored coverage, totaling 13 million additional uninsured Americans. If the data is correct, it means that there will likely be an adverse selection on the individual market, increasing insurance premiums by an average of 10% annually from 2018 to 2027.

Even though the Republicans were successful in eliminating the effects of the individual federal mandate, an increasing number of states are exploring the possibility of rolling out their own individual health coverage mandates. Several states including California have been experimenting with it, and more states are sure to follow.

However, do note that this amendment to the individual mandate does not undo any other provision of the ACA. This means that the 3.8% net investment income tax and the 0.9% Additional Medicare Tax remain intact. The current reporting requirements applicable to employers are also unaffected with the amendment to the Individual Mandate.

Chapter 8

Businesses in the New Era

The TCJA has been widely praised for being pretty supportive of businesses and corporations. The changes in taxation laws are mostly favorable toward both large and small scale businesses. All in all, most companies and their owners will be supportive and welcoming of the new amendments under the TCJA as the amendments are mostly favorable to businesses. However, some tax breaks have been reduced or removed to make room for tax cuts and other beneficial revisions. The subsequent chapters only seek to lay out the changes in taxation laws with regard to businesses and corporations. Ethical debates surrounding issues such as equality and equity will not be discussed in the book at all.

Corporate Tax in the US

The U.S. has the highest military spending in the world, which is essential in ensuring our security and to deter any malicious intent from plotting against the U.S. Since 2001, the U.S. has been pretty successful in keeping at bay any large-scale attacks. In parallel, the U.S. also has the highest corporate tax rate among all the other countries in the

Organization for Economic Co-operation and Development (OECD). Before you begin to applaud the U.S.' effort, there is a need to understand that while high military spending keeps enemies away, high corporate tax rates keep business away. The high tax rate in the U.S. has been one of the key reasons as to why companies are relocating to other countries where the tax rates are significantly lower. Such high tax rates put the U.S. in a very uncompetitive position, which exacerbates the existing trade deficit and, in turn, dragging the whole economy down as well.

One of the most prominent provisions within the TCJA is the permanent lowering of federal corporate income tax rates from 35 percent to 21 percent. The newly adjusted rate of 21% is positioned much closer to the average tax rate of the OECD countries and, as such, enhances the attractiveness of the U.S. as a location for business. A corporate income tax rate that is closer to that of other countries will discourage profit shifting to lower-tax jurisdictions which could, in turn, generate higher tax revenue for the federal government.

Ultimately, the purpose of the lowering of corporate tax is to attract investors back to the U.S. New investments stimulate the domestic economy which will, in turn, generate economic benefits for the rest of the population. New investments increase the size of capital stock, productivity, output, wages, and by extension, creates more jobs for people as well. The Tax Foundation Taxes and Growth model estimates that the total effect of the lowering of corporate tax will boost the economy by 1.7 percent, an increment of 1.5 percent in wages, a 4.8 percent larger capital stock, and 339,000 additional full-time equivalent jobs in the long term.

Corporate AMT repealed

The Alternative Minimum Tax (AMT) as described under Chapter 3 is an alternative tax computation that does not allow certain deductions or modifies the conditions for certain deductions. It used to apply to corporations as well. Let us use depreciation as an example since most corporations would almost always have depreciable assets. Depreciation can be defined as a decrease in the value of an asset over time, and there are multiple methods of calculating it. The AMT acts as a flat tax and limits the benefits of specific tax strategies. For any given year, corporations are required to pay the higher of their regular tax computation or the AMT computation. The AMT paid in prior years is available as a credit in certain situations. Before the TCJA, the corporate AMT was set at a 20% rate. However, certain corporations were exempted from the corporate AMT. These companies are usually those with average annual returns that do not exceed $7.5 million. The corporate AMT is set to be repealed for tax years beginning in 2018 or in later years. But what about corporations that have met and completed payment of the corporate AMT in previous years? In such cases, an AMT credit will be provided. The new law allows corporations to fully carry over their AMT credits and then use them in the 2018-2021 tax years or if the AMT credit depletes whichever comes first.

State and local tax changes

The greater administrative burden lies ahead as states (and

localities) grapple with conformity to the TCJA. From January 8, 2018, onwards, already more than half the states have automatically opted to review their tax laws following the amended federal Internal Revenue Code (IRC) under the TCJA. The other states, of course, will also carry out the necessary reviews in due course. However, I foresee all states to adhere to the amendments as per the TCJA. The disparity can be partly attributed to the swiftness in legislatures in amending their laws accordingly. Some states do so automatically once the TCJA kicks in, while some other states require the various provisions listed in the TCJA to undergo a round of review in their respective state legislatures. For individuals living in states of the latter, it will be essential to check out the amendments in any of the state taxation laws. This is because not all aspects of the TCJA may necessarily be adopted. In addition, even for states that have amended their state laws to the TCJA, because of a time and information gap between the federal and state levels, it would be unreasonable for individuals to expect tax laws at the state level to take effect from January 2018 as well, which is the date when the TCJA kicks in at the federal level.

Form w-4 withholding allowance certificates

From 2018 onwards, personal exemption deduction is suspended as I have previously mentioned at the beginning of this book. This stipulation, of course, will end by 2025. However, during the period whereby personal exemption is suspended, the IRS still has the right to continue to administer the income tax withholding regulations per Section 3402 for tax years before 2019. Whether the wage withholding regulations under the personal exemption will be amended or not depends on the decision of the Treasury and the IRS. From 2018 onwards, the federal income tax withholding tables will still include personal allowances, and employees do not have to submit a separate Form W-4. However, do take note that the IRS has plans to create a new Form W-4 in 2019 following the amendments made due to the TCJA. The amendment of Form W-4 will have cascaded effects on states which, at present, have been relying on the previous Form W-4 for their respective withholding laws as well.

Two provisions of the TCJA affect the payroll tax treatment of fringe benefits, and these too can affect state taxability for income tax, income tax withholding, unemployment insurance, and other state employment taxes (e.g., disability insurance). The impact on state payroll taxes is immediate in those states that conform automatically to the IRC and will change over time as other state legislatures consider conformity with these federal provisions. Here are the state taxability provisions to watch out for:

Moving Expenses. Reimbursements for moving expenses issued to employees or third parties from 2018 onwards through December 31, 2025, will not be automatically included in wages. However, members of the Armed Forces on active duty who are required to move due to a military order and incident to a permanent change of station will not be affected by this amendment.

Bicycle commuting benefits. Bicycle commuting benefits will automatically be included in the salaries of employees under Section 132(f) starting from January 1, 2018, and through December 31, 2025.

Chapter 9

Corporate Deductions

Qualified Business Income Deduction

Prior to the implementation of the TCJA, business entities such as "sole proprietorships, partnership, S corporations, and LLCs that are treated as sole proprietorships or as partnerships for tax purposes" tend to pass their net taxable income directly to the owners. This income which originally belongs to that of the business is now taxed according to individual rates. However, while the figures are passed through to the owners, it does not necessarily mean that the owners have received the cash. The subsequent example will help you to understand the problem with pass-through income better:

Company ABC has two owners, Jack and Jill who are equal partners, which means that each owns 50% of the company. According to their income statement for the year of 2018, the net income was $500,000. Jack and Jill then shared the income equally of $250,000 each. According to the law, both of them are then required to report their income as $250,000 regardless of whether they received the money. The money could be left within the company for whatever reasons that they have decided to use the money for. Assuming that Jack is liable to a 20% income tax rate, he will then be liable to pay $50,000 to the IRS even though he did not receive a single cent from the company. This is the complication of pass-through income which makes it pretty unfair for the company owners.

However, under the TCJA, multiple self-employed individuals, sole proprietors, partners in partnerships, beneficial owners of trusts, and shareholders in S corporations may be eligible for a new deduction. Referred to as Section 199A or the deduction for qualified business income will allow business owners to deduct up to 20% of their qualified business income. This deduction will commence for tax years beginning after December 31, 2017. Eligible taxpayers will claim this deduction for the first time on the 2018 federal income tax return they file in 2019.

Qualified Business Income (QBI) includes domestic income from a trade or business. It does not include employee wages, capital gain, interest, or dividend income. Essentially, you can define QBI as the "net amount of qualified items of income, gain, deduction and loss from any qualified business of the non-corporate owner." According to this definition, any item such as profits or losses related to the conduct of a business is related to QBI. QBI does not "include certain investment items, reasonable compensation paid to an owner for services rendered to the business or any guaranteed payments to a partner or LLC member treated as a partner for services rendered to the partnership or LLC." The QBI deduction is not allowed in calculating the owner's AGI, but it helps to reduce taxable income. Effectively, it should be treated similarly to that of an allowable itemized deduction.

Taxpayers whose 2018 taxable incomes fall below $315,000 for joint returns and below $157,500 for other taxpayers are eligible for the deduction. It is generally equal to the lesser of:

- 20% of their approved business earnings in addition to another 20% of their approved public partnership income and approved real estate investment trust dividends and/or

- 20% of taxable income minus net capital gains.

For businesses other than sole proprietorships, the guideline for QBI deduction is that the amount of deduction must not exceed the owner's:

- 50% of the total amount of W-2 salaries disbursed to employees

- The sum of 25% of W-2 wages plus 2.5% of the cost of qualified property.

A W-2 tax wage is the amount of taxes withheld from your employee's paycheck for the year which is then submitted to the IRS.

Qualified property is any physical property owned by a qualified business and has been operationalized in a particular tax year as part of generating the business's income.

The QBI deduction is generally not applicable for income from most professional services and businesses other than that of architecture and engineering and those that belong to the category of investment-type services. These investment-type services include such brokerages and other similar forms of investment consultant entities. With the exception set into place, the W-2 wage restriction does not come into place until an owner's taxable income, for joint filers, goes above $157,000 or alternatively, $315,000. If there is any amount that increase above the aforementioned income levels, then the W-2 wage limitation will begin to reduce by $50,000 or $100,000 for joint filers.

Reduced Dividends Received Deduction

Under pre-TCJA law, corporations that received revenue and earnings from other corporations can reduce those earnings partly. Generally, companies are entitled to a 70% rate deduction unless the company owns 20% of the stock of the company that is issuing the dividends, then an 80% deduction will apply instead. However, with the TCJA, the 70% and 80% rate has been adjusted to 50% and 65% respectively.

Primarily, the Dividends Received Deduction (DRD) is a federal write-off in the U.S. which applies to certain corporations that receive dividends from affiliated entities. This deduction seeks to minimize the dire consequences of triple taxation. Triple taxation happens when the same income is taxed three times: (1) in the hands of the company paying the dividends, (2) then the receiving company of these dividends, (3) and finally when the shareholder is paid a dividend.

The DRD permits a company that receives dividends from another company to deduct those dividends from its income and, therefore, reduces its income tax as per the deduction.

However, there are certain technicalities and rules involved for the corporate shareholders to be eligible to the DRD. The amount of DRD that a company is entitled to depend on the company's percentage of ownership in the company that is distributing the dividend.

There are three layers in determining the number of possible deductions. First, as a rule of thumb, the amount of DRD a company is entitled to be equivalent to 70% of the dividends received. Second, if the receiving company owns more than 20% but less than 80% of the company paying the dividend, the DRD surmounts to 80% of the number of issued dividends. Finally, if the receiving company owns more than 80% of the company paying the dividend, the DRD equates to 100% of the number of dividends paid out.

Do take note that taxable income limitations also apply to DRD provisions. Under this rule, which affects dividends of the receiving companies in which the payee has less than 80% ownership, the DRD equals 70% or 80% of its taxable income if the taxable income of the receiving corporation is lower than what the DRD would have been. However, the effects of the taxable income limitation will be voided if the DRD results or adds on to a net operating loss.

Another fundamental technical rule is that to justify the basis in claiming the DRD, the receiving company must have ownership over the shares of the paying company for a minimum of 45 days before the date of issuance of dividends.

Assume that XYZ Inc. owns 60% of its affiliate ABC Inc. Under a scenario whereby the dividends received by XYZ is lower than its net taxable income, the following example will apply. If XYZ has a net taxable income of $10,000 which includes $9,000 received as dividends from ABC, it would be entitled to a DRD of $7,200, or 80% of $9,000.

Let us assume a different scenario whereby the dividends received is higher than the net taxable income. If XYZ's net taxable income is $9,000 which includes a dividend amount of $10,000, then the income limitation rule mentioned in the earlier paragraphs would apply. This means that the DRD that XYZ is applicable for will no longer be 80% of the dividends received but rather 80% of the net taxable income.

Business Related Exclusions and Deductions

The TCJA has put in place a ceiling on business interest expense. This limit is inapplicable if a business's average annual gross receipts are $25 million or less for the three preceding tax years.

If a business fulfills the requirements on this ceiling, this change will only kick in for taxable years from December 31, 2017, onwards. The business interest deduction ceiling for a taxable year is the culmination of:

- Business interest income

- 30% of the adjusted taxable income, and

- Floor plan financing interest expense, if the business does have one.

The sum of any business interest expense that is disallowed as a deduction for the taxable year will be brought forward to the subsequent year as a disallowed business interest expense carry forward.

A partnership that is affected by the business interest limit applies that limit at the partnership level. The partnership does not carry forward any disallowed business interest expense but allocates the disallowed amount to the individual partners. A partner can deduct the disallowed carry forward business interest expense in the following year if the partner meets the requirements in the following year.

A taxpayer involved in a real property trade or business or a farming business may elect not to limit business interest expense. This is an irreversible election. A business that makes this election will have to use the alternative depreciation system and is not eligible for the special depreciation allowance for that property. For a taxpayer with more than one qualifying business, the election is made for each trade of business.

Certain utility trades or businesses will not be affected by the business interest expense limitation.

The instructions for the new Form 8990 include definitions related to this topic and can help taxpayers calculate the amount of business interest expense they can deduct and the amount they can carry forward to the next year.

Charitable Contribution Deduction

From 2018 onwards, the stipulations that affect a trust will no longer apply to charitable contribution deductions of an Electing Small Business Trust (ESBT). An ESBT will determine its deduction based on individual taxpayer rules.

To calculate the deduction, the ESBT has to first determine its AGI. This will be calculated similar to that of an individual, except for the fact that deductions are allowed for administrative costs of the ESBT which does not apply to individuals. The deduction will have also included the price of the property having being held in an ESBT.

Like-Kind Exchanges of Real Property

In general, when a taxpayer enters into the transaction of changing businesses or investments for the sole reason of receiving other businesses or investments of a like or similar kind, they will not need to register a gain or a loss.

However, the TCJA has set restrictions on like-kind exchange treatment only to specific exchanges of real property excluding personal or intangible property. An exchange of real property held solely for sale still does not fit the criteria as a like-kind exchange. To justify an exchange as a like-kind exchange, the taxpayer must possess the real property for productive uses such as that of a business or investment. A transition provision in the TCJA states that Section 1031 affects qualifying exchanges of personal or intangible property if the taxpayer disposed the exchanged property before January 01, 2018, or received replacement property before that date. Thus, effective from January 1, 2018, onwards, exchanges of collectibles, patents, vehicles, machinery, artwork, other intellectual property, and intangible business assets usually are not eligible for non-recognition of gain or loss as that like-kind exchanges. However, certain exchanges of a mutual ditch, irrigation stock, or reservoir are still eligible for non-recognition of gain or loss as like-kind exchanges.

Qualified Bicycle Commuting Reimbursement

Before the TCJA, an exclusion from wages for federal income tax, federal income tax withholding, Social Security/Medicare and federal unemployment insurance purposes applied to qualified bicycle commuting expenses of up to $20 every month amid which the worker frequently utilizes the bike for a significant part of traveling among home and work. The prohibition does not make a difference around the same time the worker gets other transportation incidental advantages from the business (e.g., vanpool, transit pass, parking on the employer's premises).

With the TCJA, bicycle commuting benefits reimbursed to employees on and after January 1, 2018, and through December 31, 2025, are included in their salaries.

Employers will need to be sure that they pay all bicycle commuting benefits owed for the tax year 2017, on or before December 31, 2018. Do bear in mind that without IRS guidance otherwise, benefits paid on, and after January 1, 2018, are included in wages even if related to benefits earned in 2017.

Employers are required to amend their tax configuration settings for earning to reflect the inclusion of bicycle commuting benefits in wages. There will also be a comparable amendment for state and local income tax on withholding purposes, especially for those states that conform to the IRC as of January 1, 2018.

Meals, entertainment, and transportation

The law permits a 100% deduction for businesses for de minimis meal expenses incurred. De minimis refers to something that is too small or insignificant to be of any importance to the business, such that "accounting for it would be unreasonable or administratively impracticable." The law states that the operations by an employer of any eating facility can be considered as de minimis if the following criteria apply:

- Revenue derived from the facility usually tallies or surpasses the facility's immediate and direct operation costs.

- The facility is located within or near the business premises of the employers.

To determine if the revenue derived from the facility usually meets or increases beyond operating costs established by it, and employee will be provided the opportunity to remove the cost of food that is provided at this facility. It will be considered that paying for such meals is equivalent to the operating costs incurred by the facility.

The law provides that the meals provided to employees and their spouses and dependents are excluded from gross income if provided for the inconvenience of the employer on or near the employer's business premises. The law also states that all meals given to employees within business premises by an employer will be perceived as for the convenience of the employer if such meals make up more than 50% of the total meals given.

The law further provides that a de minimis benefit also

includes property or service given to workers if the intrinsic value (after considering the frequency with which the employer issues similar fringes to employees) is so insignificant as to make accounting for it unreasonable or administratively impracticable.

The IRS includes meals as an exempt de minimis fringe benefit:

- In the case of a meal or money, such benefits are given to sustain an employee to work overtime. Thus, for example, meals issued or money provided to the employee to purchase food within the employer's premises and these meals are consumed while the employee is working overtime satisfies this condition.

- Meals or money given that is provided to an employee because overtime work requires the employee to put in efforts beyond the agreed timetable established for said employee. This condition will always be met because the circumstances giving rise to the need for overtime work are reasonably foreseeable.

- Meals or money given to an employee on an occasional basis.

The TCJA modifies the law such that the business deduction for de minimis meals and meals given, that serves the convenience of the employer at or near the employer's business premises to be limited to 50%. The IRS clarifies in Publication 15-B that meal expenses which is provided to the employee during recreational activities or events, such as company events and holidays, are not subjected to this 50% deduction limit (meaning, a 100% deduction is allowed). However, a 100% deduction is only permissible when these meal expenses are provided mainly to assist the employees.

These employees do include those who have a significant share in the employer's business, or other highly compensated employees. Note that the federal payroll tax treatment of eating facilities and de minimis meals remain the same as before.

In view of the fall in business deductions to 50% for expenses incurred from now through December 31, 2025, and the overall loss of the business deduction effective January 1, 2026, employers will need to think about the changes in policies, if any, that affect free meals served to employees to make it more convenient for the employer and also with regard to the operation of their on-premises eating facilities. IRS guidance is necessary to comprehend better how the business deduction is computed when revenues of on-premises eating facilities equate or surpass its real operating costs. IRS guidance is required to fully comprehend the cascading effects of the TCJA on other de minimis meals including overtime meals and supper money.

Employee achievement awards

The pre-TCJA era provides an exclusion from wages for an employer-provided length of service and safety achievement awards. The exclusion is capped to $400 per employee per year if there is no appropriate plan and up to $1,600 under a recognized plan with the average exclusion to be limited to $400 per employee. Other limitations apply. For instance, a length of service award is excluded from taxable wages only once every five years. The law also stipulated that the award must be an item of personal, tangible property (e.g., a watch, ring, or other transactional items). The IRS clarifies that the exclusion does not affect items of intangible personal property including cash, cash equivalents including gift certificates, gift cards, or other intangible property such as meals, vacations, lodging, tickets to sporting or theater events, bonds, stocks, and other securities.

In effect from January 1, 2018, the TCJA clarifies that qualified recognized employee achievements, prizes can be given that are in the form of cash, cash equivalents including gift certificates, gift cards or coupons (less agreements benefiting the power to choose and be awarded with certain forms of property, whereby such properties already selected and approved by the employer), or lodgings, meals, vacations, tickets to sporting or theater events, bonds, stocks, other securities, and other similar items.

Employers should consider promulgating their policy of permitting sheer items regarding physical personal property for length-of-service and safety awards to every manager and supervisor to prevent uncalculated taxable awards. If you have, all along even prior to 2018, been providing employees items other than tangible personal property, and you have yet to include them in federal taxable wages, consider if you can protect yourself from future IRS audit assessments by revealing the taxable wages and paying the owed taxes using Form 941-X and issuing/filing Form W-2c. You might also want to think about state and local voluntary disclosures. Employers should also review their length-of-service and safety achievement policies. If you are currently issuing things such as intangible personal property (e.g., gift certificates, vacations, gift cards), determine if this practice will continue moving ahead.

Entertainment expenses

Before 2017, deductions for expenses relating to amusement, entertainment, or recreational activities and facilities were not allowed, unless the item pertains to or related to the business. This usually means that the deduction is allowed if there was a substantial and bona fide business discussion just before or right after the amusement, entertainment, or recreation event. For these purposes, more recreational activities are perceived as included under the overarching umbrella of amusement, entertainment, or recreation. The disallowance has to fulfill specific requirements, including food and beverages for employees provided within the business premises; reimbursed expenses; expenses treated as compensation; business meetings for employees; nondiscriminatory recreation for employees; agents or directors; stockholders; items available to the public; entertainment sold to customers; and business league meetings.

If an entertainment expense is exempted from disallowance by any exceptions or due to the direct relation of the expense to or associated with business, it is generally permitted at the deduction rate of 50% of the expense. This 50% disallowance also affects deductible expenses for meals. An entertainment or meal expense is exempted from the 50% disallowance under certain exceptions, such as if the expense is considered as compensation, or as previously stated, then the cost of the meal can be subtracted from the employee's income.

From January 1, 2018, it is not permissible for businesses to claim a deduction for entertainment expenses or a facility or portion thereof used for these activities, even if directly related to or associated with the conduct of business.

The 50% deduction ceiling that used to apply to meals and entertainment expenses is now limited solely to meal expenses. This change usually makes sense within the framework of the statutory charge because business deduction disallowance now understandably forbids entertainment expenses without regard to whether the expense is associated with a trade or business.

Hence, all forms of business entertainment including fishing, golf outings, sporting events, sailings, resort events, and theaters are likely to be entirely non-deductible moving forward even if substantial and bona fide business discussions were affiliated with the activity.

There may, however, be a separate portion within the existing pie of entertainment expenses that are exempted from the deduction disallowance by certain exceptions – such as business meetings of employees, agents, stockholders, or directors and meetings of business leagues.

Therefore, the employer must establish general ledger accounts that are sufficient in spotting entertainment expenses where the business deduction is forbidden - those that apply to the 50% deduction limits, and those where a 100% deduction is permitted. For example, different general ledger accounts are required for (1) a theater event for an employee where a 100% business subtraction is permitted, (2) meal expenses incurred for a business meeting or as a travel expense where a 50% deduction limits applies, and (3) a theater event for a customer where a business deduction is not permitted.

Businesses will have to reconsider how deduction disallowance for certain entertainment events and the corresponding facilities will affect their business expense policy and subsequently cascade down to business entertainment policies. If entertainment expense reimbursement is added in the employee's taxable wages (and since 100% deductions are permitted for compensation expenses), consider if federal income tax and FICA taxes will be paid on behalf of employees (gross-up). Also, think about including an earnings code to the payroll system for capturing reimbursed entertainment expenses because they may be exempted from state and local income tax (e.g., those states that do not abide by the IRC amendments as of January 1, 2018).

Transportation fringe benefits

Businesses are allowed to remove all of the expenses incurred in providing transportation fringes under Section 132(f). Specifically, it allows for exclusion from wages for qualified vanpools, qualified parking at or near the workplace, and transit benefits. For 2018, the exclusion from taxable wages is $260 per month for vanpools/transit passes and $260 for parking. Under Section 132(f)(3), employers may establish a system whereby employees can purchase their transportation fringes with pre-tax expenses up to the stipulated monthly limit. Pretax contributions for transportation fringe benefits are subtracted from wages.

Effective January 1, 2018, Section 274 has been amended to such that no deduction is permitted for any expense incurred due to supplying of transportation or any payment or reimbursement for transportation fringe benefits in Section 132(f) except as necessary to ensure the safety of the employee.

The deduction disallowance has no effects on the bicycle-commuting benefits as defined in Section 132(f)(5)(f) incurred inclusive of January 1, 2018, onwards, and after December 31, 2025. This is because, under the TCJA, bicycle-commuting benefits are integrated within wages, hence the exception. Note that it remains the same in the federal payroll tax treatment of employee parking and transit benefits. In publication 15-8, the IRS clarifies that no deduction is permitted for recognized transportation benefits, regardless of whether it was given directly by the business, through a substantial repayment agreement, or through a compensation deduction arrangement (pretax commitment) accrued or paid after December 31, 2017. Additionally, no subtraction is considered for any expense brought about for supplying any transportation, or any redistribution to employees with regard to movement between an employee's home and office, aside from guaranteeing the wellbeing of the worker, or for qualified bike driving repayments as portrayed in area 132(f)(5)(f) (despite the fact that the non-inclusion from federal taxable wages for qualified bicycle commuting reimbursements is suspended). IRS guidance will be necessary as follow:

- Parking – free lots. IRS guidance is needed to confirm if a deduction is disallowed according to parking lots if costs incurred by the employer where parking spaces are free at no charge to customers and employees

- Parking – customer and employee shared lots. IRS advice is required to calculate the deduction disallowance for parking lots located at or near the business premises that are free to both customers and employees.

In light of the deduction disallowance for transportation fringe benefits, business will need to decide if they will pursue a policy of issuing transportation fringe benefits to their employees. In this decision-making process, do bear in mind that certain areas demand that employers provide transportation fringe benefits to their employees.

Exempted organizations should consult with their tax-exempt organization advisor about the requirement to include transportation fringe benefit costs in unrelated business income.

Wage advances and repayments

As the claim-of-right doctrine states, special tax rules are applicable when a taxpayer must compensate a certain amount of their salary received in a prior tax year. These special tax rules can, at times, increase the amount of federal income taxes an employee is required to pay.

Specifically, if an employee is given wages in one tax year and is yet required to repay the employer in subsequent tax years, and assuming that this wage repayment is $3,000 or less, or the employee knew that it is compulsory to repay the salaries regardless of the sum, the employee is permitted to include an adjustment (i.e., credit) to his or her federal taxable income to the point that the sum of repayment surpasses 2% of the employee's adjusted gross income also known as the 2% floor.

When the wage repayment is higher than $3,000 or the employee did not realize the need to repay, the employee can claim a federal income tax refund by filing an itemized deduction in the tax year of repayment. However, the success of deduction is subjected to the 2% floor or a federal tax credit, whichever is most beneficial.

Effective January 1, 2018, and through December 31, 2025, Section 67 is amended such that all miscellaneous itemized deductions accessible to individual taxpayers for employee unreimbursed business expenses (e.g., tools of the trade, uniforms and wage repayments based on the requirements of the claim-of-right doctrine), currently subjected to the 2% floor, are disallowed entirely.

Businesses should scrutinize their wage-advance policies as they are related to employee repayments that will not be made in the tax year of 2017. Minimally, employees should be made known of the federal income tax implications of wage-advance repayments made in years after when the advance was paid.

Chapter 10

Equity Compensation Stock and RSU

The value of the property provided in recognition of the performance of services that is more than the cost of the property is embedded in an employee's gross income as long as the risk of the property getting confiscated remains low.

This provision applies as well to the transfer of stocks of either a public or private company. For stock option awards, the employee will have to include the intrinsic value of the transferred shared into his or her gross income. The intrinsic value will be as per the value of the stock on the option exercise date over the cost of the exercising.

For restricted stock units (RSUs), the employee will include the intrinsic value of shares into their gross income the moment of RSUs following vesting.

Employees who receive stock options and RSUs while working in private companies are usually liable to a higher taxable income when the stock option is being exercised or when the RSU is settled. Some companies do allow their employees to sell the withholding shares back to the company to offset the amount of taxes that these employees are liable for. However, should the company not possess such a policy to buy back shares, the employee will end up not having a choice but to cough out the additional amount of liable taxes.

Federal Income Tax Deferral Election

In order to protect employees falling under the latter category, the TCJA has created a Federal Income Tax Deferral Election for certain qualified employees who possess company stocks options and RSUs. Under this new provision, the employee can exercise his or her right to defer federal income tax whenever the stock option gets exercised or the RSU gets settled. By doing so, the employer will become liable to pay the corresponding amount of federal taxes. Otherwise, the employer will not be able to claim a business deduction. The amount of time that an employee has from the date that the RSU is transferred and the stock option is exercised to defer federal income tax is 30 days. The moment this election is made, the liable amount of federal income tax will be fixed at the point when the election is made. The amount of payable federal taxes will be delayed to a minimum of five years from the date that the shares are transferrable, which means that the shares can be publicly traded. This amount will also be embedded in the employee's federal taxable income from the date that the employee no longer works for the company or he or she chooses to nullify the election. The election will not apply to employees if they had already elected previously or when the company has already repurchased or offered to buy back the stocks.

Employees that qualify can delay their federal income tax based on the value of their shares. As long as the value of these shares is not taxed, the employer is unable to claim the deduction. While this may seem disadvantageous for the employer, from a business point of view, it may be advantageous as the employer does not have the right nor is the employer obliged to buy back the shares from the employee, ultimately improving the free cash flow of the business.

RSUs are only issued by corporations that have been private since their initiation (including preceding corporations). For RSUs to be included in the deferral election, there must be 80% or more U.S. employees that are being issued with the stock of the same weight and status, and that the amount of issued stock must be a significant sum.

Limitations of the deferral election

Not all stock options and RSUs issued are eligible for the deferral election. Only those that are related to the service industry will be eligible. Qualified stock includes incentive stock options (ISO) or an option under an employee stock purchase plan (ESPP), but an election would disqualify the ISO or the ESPP option. The restricted stock does not necessarily include a put right nor will one necessarily be able to convert the stock into cash once it is vested.

The four highest-paid officers within the company including the CEO and CFO as well as those who have ownership powers of 1% of the company do not possess the privilege to make the federal income tax deferral election on any stock option or RSU. Other than this group of people, all other full-time employees have the right to make the election. Of course, the employees have to abide and adhere to the income tax withholding rules on the restricted stock.

During vesting, the employer has to prove the quality of the stock to his or her employees. Subsequently, the employer has to make known to their employees with regard to their: (a) election rights; (b) the amount upon vesting will be locked in as taxable amount income that is irrelevant of the value of the stock; and (c) that the amount will be incurring the federal income tax withholding which will be calculated based on the individual rate of 37% which is the highest rate. Should the employer fail to fulfill any of the steps as mentioned earlier, he or she will be liable to a $100 penalty for every missing item, capped at a total of $50,000 annually.

The federal taxable income should be perceived as a non-cash fringe benefit, giving the employee more time and liberty when it comes to income tax withholding. During the process of an election, the employee's Form W-2, box 12 has to note down (1) the sum that is being disputed in the election which should be excluded from the payable income tax; (2) the sum that is already within the federal taxable income due to the election; and (3) the average amount currently deferred by the employee pursuant to all active elections. This clause is technically self-implementing without any form of intervention and may be applied by employers using a reasonable, proper faith interpretation of the statute.

The IRS explicitly states in publication 15-B that the election only has a direct impact for matters regarding federal income taxes. There is no impact on matters relating to Medicare, the application of Social Security, and federal unemployment insurance taxes. An employer usually withholds federal income tax at the rate of 37%, and this withheld amount is embedded in the wage of the employee. If conducted in such a manner that it is an optional exercise, then that option will not be included and allowed to be used as a stock option.

Action steps

Companies can adopt the following steps given the aforementioned amendments: (1) when making this determination, take the following into account- private entities offering stock options or RSUs to a broad-based group that is interested in compensating employees with stock may find the amendments advantageous to qualified employees and businesses; (2) private entities that create stock options or programs tailored specifically to qualify for the election will have to influence and convince their employees on the advantages of the federal income tax deferral election. A way to do so could be via the route of increment in share value, whereby employees will gain capital increment on any increase in the intrinsic value after exercising an option or the issuance of the RSU. Of course, as a responsible employer, you have to explain to your employees the downsides of the election. The disadvantage of it is such that under the scenario that the value of the share decreases after the exercising of the options or RSU issuance, the employee would be liable for tax calculated upon the original values of the shares before the transfer.

Chapter **11**

Executive compensation

Before the TCJA, there is a deduction limit of $1 million per tax year on the total sum of compensations reimbursed to a public company's "covered employees," which include the CEO. The $1 million deduction threshold applies to all sorts of compensations that would have been deductible in any year that is reimbursed to a covered employee at the close of that tax year. Therefore, reimbursements given after an individual is no longer a covered employee (such as termination and other delayed compensation payments) will not be part of the $1 million deduction limit.

However, there are special concessions for performance-driven compensations such as cash, stock options, and stock appreciation rights. These compensations, of course, will be dependent upon achieving specific Key Performance Indexes (KPIs) and the fulfillment of other requirements. Amounts that constitute performance-based compensation are not included in the $1 million deduction threshold. A key thing for companies to note is that only publicly-traded companies that are legally bound to register their common stock under the Securities Exchange Act are pegged to the deduction threshold of $1 million every tax year. This limit does not apply to other companies that register debt, that voluntarily register their common stock, or that are foreign private issuers' trade on U.S. exchanges via American Depository

Receipts (ADRs).

Effects of the TCJA

With the TCJA kicking in, the deduction limitation of $1 million compensation is expanded for covered employees. A transition rule is applied in this case. According to it, individuals can get compensated if it is mentioned within a legally binding contract that has been in effect inclusively since November 2, 2017. Let me further elaborate on a legally written binding contract.

The TCJA removes the idea and practice of compensation that is given based on performance. Its aim is to broaden the understanding of the phrase "covered employees." "Covered employees" include any past individual who was covered even if the individual no longer holds that post anymore. The moment an individual is labeled as a covered employee, the deduction limitation will apply to the claimable sum of reimbursement. In addition to the existing definition, it is also important to note that an individual that has been labeled as a covered employee after December 31, 2016, will continue to be labeled as such for all subsequent years.

The TCJA has also widened the scope of a public company to encompass more entities. At present, the definition of a public company will include other securities registrants, such as foreign private issuers, and even private companies. However, there is a caveat for these private companies for them to qualify as a public company. These private companies have to register their debt offerings and must report under the Securities Exchange Act.

The transition rule exempts any compensation paid "under a written binding contract [that] was in effect on November 2, 2017, and [that] was not modified in any material respect on or after such date." This transition rule applies to all material aspects with respect to the transition rule included in the statute when it was first implemented in 1993. That rule provided that "the term 'applicable employee remuneration' shall not include any remuneration payable under a written binding contract that was in effect on February 17, 1993, and [that] was not modified after that in any material respect before such remuneration is paid."

The Conference Agreement and 'Grandfathered' Laws

The Conference Agreement

As mentioned above, it is clearly stated in the Conference Agreement of the TCJA that a predetermined and contracted compensation fits critical criteria as an exception. The criteria are such that the predetermined sum of compensation is included in a legally and written binding contract which includes the insured employee, and this contract has to be in effect inclusively from November 2, 2017.

Nevertheless, this does not mean that any contract drafted since this date is sufficed in justifying the legality of that contract. For example, an injured employee has signed a legally written binding contract with his or her employer since November 2, 2017. Within the contract, it states that the employee has the right to claim his or her rightful compensation at a later date of which the sum has been determined in the contract. However, this contract is lacking a crucial detail. The contract must explicitly state that the employer will not have the right, under whatsoever conditions, to change the amount of compensation or to nullify the contract (unless under specific circumstances). Without this clause stated explicitly within the contract, it gives the employer the liberty to "grandfather" the payments clause which will not be fair to the individual employee.

The Conference Agreement does not address what constitutes a material modification of a contract or the extent of modification required such that the amended contract is now considered a fresh contract. The Treasury Department and IRS have to implode into the existing regulations, which include detailed rules on what constitutes a material modification. Under regulations, material modification occurs when the contract is amended to increase the sum of compensation to the employee. The modification can also refer to the employer amending the method of payment or a verbal sideline agreement between the employer and the employee.

Grandfathering of Laws

Primarily, since existing regulations are probably going to remain as they are, the Treasury and the IRS are likely to base their interpretations and judgments on these regulations with regard to terms like modification, written binding contracts, and grandfathering of laws. Given all these clauses and provisions, the key question that companies would have in their heads would be how these clauses would affect them?

Once the law has been passed, the public companies have to assess and make the decision almost instantaneously as to the number of compensation awards that have been exempted from the $1 million deduction threshold but does not apply under the new establishment. This process of sieving out the various compensation awards requires a bit more time in interpreting the November 2, 2017, grandfather rule and its impact on the company's existing compensation policies. There needs to be a more explicit analysis and interpretation for every single plan or contract. Once companies have done so, they will realize that the grandfather rule is more limiting than enabling, contrary to initial predictions, which was based on a brief interpretation of the provisions and clauses listed in the Conference Agreement.

The battle between the single individual seeking enforcement of reimbursement as of November 2, 2017, and the arrangement between the intricate nature underlying contracts and the employment law will determine whether a binding contract between the employer and employee would be the way forward. It is apparent that the right to discontinue the service of an employee or to change the terms within a contract is stated clearly in the Conference Agreement, and thus, this suggests that the Conference Agreement is not the ghost of the past. An agreement which has an incentive-driven compensation plan cannot be grandfathered under the new provision because for the latter, and the company has the right to amend the contract or otherwise the ability to renege on previously agreed compensations.

If employers are adopting the elucidation as mentioned

earlier into the transition rule, then the transition rule would be hardly enforceable unless the employer decides and legally agrees that the negative discretion was unfeasible and unforeseeable, and, therefore, the employee is rightfully liable to the designated amount of compensation.

Other possible questions may be asked about plans or arrangements that may be canceled subsequently and which part of the delayed reimbursement sum accrued under the plan or arrangement after the effective date is grandfathered. The Conference Agreement clarifies that when a contract is cancelable by either party (excluding a cancellation purely by the employee's decisions to quit), then the contract will be deemed as a fresh contract with a date stamp on the date that the cancellation took place. For example, assume an executive is participating in a delayed compensation policy that is crafted in such a way to pay out after the executive leaves employment. Under existing law, the plan fails to fulfill the requirements for the $1 million deduction restriction because post-employment payments are excluded. It is pretty standard for plans of this sort to include provisions such that the company can cancel its plan considerably during any point in time. This means that a company can retain the right to stop or cancel accrual under the plan subsequently, as long as the sums accumulated through that date are not subtracted. If such a clause were added in the plan document, then a simple glance over the grandfather rule would imply that only the account balance as of November 2, 2017, is grandfathered. Such can be inferred because, in theory, the employer could stop or terminate the plan subsequently on any date after November 2, 2017. Once again, an employer should seek to understand precisely if underlying employment laws would require such termination to fit the transition clause of the grandfather provision for benefits earned after November 2, 2017.

The Conference Agreement contains the exact words that can be found in the committee reports when the legislation was initially ratified in 1993. However, in 1993, there was a policy rationale to restrict the transition rule and implement the written binding contract exception with extra caution because Congress wanted to incentivize employers to implement performance-based policies instantly and to terminate all other previous agreements whatever they may be. Such a policy rationale is not present under the TCJA because the performance-based compensation exemption is being eliminated.

More positively, termination provisions are pretty uncommon under certain types of equity grants such as a genuine appreciation grants or stock option. In these cases, grants claimed before November 3, 2017, have a high chance that they will continue to be grandfathered. However, an assessment of the provisions is needed to affirm the analysis. The Conference Agreement also stated that a criterion to carry out subsequent services is not a restriction to grandfather treatment; therefore, if a compensation grant is conditional only due to the employee's continuation in carrying out similar services in the future (i.e., it is not vested), that condition itself does not restrict grandfather treatment, provided that the grant was claimed on the required date. Given the cascading effect that the Conference Agreement has, and the way that it was written, subsequent clarifications from the Treasury and IRS are required for determining what constitutes a written binding contract. It will be crucial for companies to keep an eye on these developments. Moving ahead, amendments have to be made to show compliance. Companies will need to track a prospectively increasing group of covered employees that are eligible within the $1 million compensation deduction threshold. On top of adding the CFO to the covered employee group beginning in the tax year 2018, over a sustained period, the affected group will develop beyond the existing covered top five officers as a result of the "once a covered employee, always a covered employee" rule.

What should companies do?

Organizations that are currently not liable to IRC Section 162(m) must observe the suggested expansion of criteria on businesses that may eventually fall under the compensation deduction limitation. Specifically, companies whose primary operations are outside of the U.S. should reconsider the length to which the deduction limit affects their tax returns in the U.S., even when they are perceived as a publicly-traded company for per Section 162(m). For example, prospective covered employees could also be hired in non-U.S. jurisdictions (suggesting that no U.S. deduction will reduce their compensations if any). More advice is required to properly review and confirm the specific application of IRC Section 162(m) to such companies.

Finally, companies have to rethink how they wish to organize their senior executive compensation programs given the abolishment of the performance-based reimbursement exception clause under Section 162(m). Without a doubt, the effects of performance-based programs will continue for multiple non-tax reasons; companies may not be required to add some of the more rigid or process-oriented clauses that were stated to sustain the compensation deduction provision based on the Section 162(m) definition of a performance-based compensation plan. Companies may also want to pay more emphasis to possible structures that could preserve more of the compensation deduction. For example, in place of bounties over $1 million upon termination of employment service, compensation stipends made over periods that sum up to less than $1 million per year permits for a corporate deduction. There are two main things that business owners can do: (1) Speak to your exempt-organization tax advisor. It will be essential to talk to your exempt-organization tax advisor about the latest updates to include non-deductible executive compensation in unaffiliated business income; or (2) speak to your compensation and benefits advisor. It will be essential to talk to compensation and welfare professional about the technicalities of the business deduction threshold for executive compensation, and how these amendments may affect your business compensation-related policies subsequently.

Chapter **12**

Depreciations

Accelerated Depreciation

Accelerated depreciation is the most substantial corporate tax break, allowing companies to deduct the costs of assets faster than their value declines. Depreciation is the most significant component in the corporate tax code and is broadly enjoyed by most, if not all enterprises.

To make sense of accelerated depreciation, it is essential first to understand that U.S. businesses are taxed on profits – meaning to say their revenues after deducting their expenses. Because many large expenses including purchases of equipment and buildings are used throughout decades to produce income, these items have to be depreciated over their respective life determined by the class they are in. It is, however, impractical to determine the actual life of every asset. Thus, the tax code groups various types of assets into sets of "class lives" and gives each a "schedule" – the number of years during which the particular asset must be depreciated to account for tax purposes, as opposed to subtracting the full cost when first purchased. Accelerated depreciation, therefore, allows assets to be depreciated exponentially as compared to a straight-line depreciation whereby the amount of depreciation yearly is the same.

The Modified Accelerated Cost Recovery System (MACRS) which was implemented in 1986 is a method of depreciation that uses accelerated depreciation. Companies have been dependent on the MACRS to tap into the benefits of accelerated depreciation. The main feature of the MACRS which qualifies it as providing exponential acceleration is it shortens class lives, resulting in depreciation to take place quicker, and give companies the opportunity to deduct more of an item's initial cost in the earlier years. Alternatively, companies can adopt the Alternative Depreciation System - which more accurately reflects economic depreciation - extending the class lives that each item has, and uses a straight-line depreciation method, meaning that depreciation cost is the same annually.

With a quicker depreciation timeline, companies can apply for higher expenses and thus reduce their short-term taxable income. Although a company theoretically pays the same amount of tax since the life of the asset remains the same, an earlier deduction of their taxable income permits companies to take advantage of "the time value of money," reaping higher interest savings, increased cash flow, and higher investments returns. Effective tax rates due to accelerated depreciation differ mostly based on the different types of assets but are biased towards investments in equipment.

Legislative History of the Two Expensing Allowances

There are two central legislation sections that one has to care about with regard to depreciation or expensing allowances – Section 179 and Section 168.

Section 179[1] expensing allowance has been a permanent feature of the federal tax code since September 1958. It started as a first-year depreciation allowance that Congress included in the Small Business Tax Revision Act of 1958. Its purpose then was the same as it is today: to reduce the tax liability for small business owners to stimulate small business investment and simplify tax accounting for smaller firms. The original deduction was capped at $2,000 ($4,000 for a married couple filing a joint return) for the cost of new and second-hand business machines and equipment with a tax life of six or more years that were purchased and operationalize (to put in service) in a particular tax year.

No amendments were made in the allowance until the enactment of the Economic Recovery Tax Act of 1981 (ERTA). The ERTA increased the dispensing allowance to $5,000 and came out with a timetable for a gradual increment in the dispensing allowance to $10,000 in 1986. Even with the 150% increase in the allowance for single filers, few firms took it to their liberty, which was a strange phenomenon. Some attributed the tepid response to the limitation on the utilization of an investment tax credit that ERTA built up. A business taxpayer could secure the investment tax credit just for the part of an asset that meets the requirements and was not expensed, so the total credit could be utilized only if the organization asserted no expensing stipend. For some organizations, the sum of tax funds saved from the credit exceeded the sum of tax funds from a blend of the credit and the stipend.

To prevent the ascent into government spending deficiency in the mid-1980s, Congress passed the Deficit Reduction Act of 1984. In addition to other things, the act delayed from 1986 to 1990 the scheduled increment in the expensing stipend to $10,000. In any case, utilization of the recompense climbed extraordinarily following the nullification of the investment tax credit by the Tax Reform Act of 1986.

The stipend rose to $10,000 in 1990 as scheduled and stayed at that dimension until the entry of the Omnibus Budget Reconciliation Act of 1993 (OBRA93). The OBRA93 increased the allowance to $17,500 and created a variety of tax benefits for impoverished areas known as "enterprise" zones and "empowerment" zones (or EZs for short). The benefits include an enhanced expensing allowance for qualified assets placed in service in such a zone. To be designated an EZ, an area has to meet specific requirements which include poverty rate, geographic size, and population.

With the passing of the Small Business Job Protection Act of 1996, the regular expensing allowance was once again scheduled for timely increases. Specifically, the act increased the stipend to "$18,000 in 1997, $18,500 in 1998, $19,000 in 1999, $20,000 in 2000, $24,000 in 2001 and 2002 similarly, and $25,000 in 2003 and subsequent years."

The Community Renewal Tax Relief Act of 2000 included "renewal communities" (RCs) to the existing list of economic development areas and provided businesses located in them equal tax benefits which are available to businesses in EZs including an enhanced expensing allowance. Also, it added a premium of $35,000 to the regular allowance for qualified assets placed in service in economic development areas.

September 11

To reduce the economic crisis related to the terrorist attacks of September 11, 2001, Congress set up an assortment of tax breaks through the Job Creation and Worker Assistance Act of 2002. The advantages were planned to empower new business interest in the areas located in lower Manhattan in New York City that was central to the brunt of the terror assaults on the World Trade Center. Proprietors of firms situated in the "Liberty Zone" were permitted to secure the equivalent upgraded expensing stipend for qualified projects that was accessible to business owners in the EZs and RCs.

After the Small Business Job Protection Act of 1996 (SBJPA), no progressions were offered in the standard allowance until the Jobs and Growth Tax Reduction and Reconciliation Act of 2003 (JGTRRA). With the demonstration, the remittance rose four-crease to $100,000 and remained at that sum in 2004 and 2005 before getting reset in 2006 and beyond at its level before JGTRRA ($25,000). JGTRRA also raised the phase-out limit to $400,000 from May 2003 until December 31, 2005. The JGTRRA also indexed the regular allowance and the phase-out limit for inflation in both 2004 and 2005 and included off-the-shelf software for business use to the list of depreciable assets liable for expenses in the same period. The American Jobs Creation Act of 2004 extended the changes made by JGTRRA through the end of 2007.

Hurricane Katrina

To facilitate the recovery of the economies in the devastated areas of Louisiana, Mississippi, and Alabama that were struck by Hurricane Katrina in 2005, Congress passed the Gulf Opportunity Zone Act of 2005. Among various provisions, the act created a "Gulf Opportunity Zone" (GOZ) in these disaster-stricken areas and provided a series of tax breaks and incentives to boost business investment in the GOZ. This includes an enhanced expensing stipend for qualified assets purchased on or after August 28, 2005, and operationalized (placed in service) by December 31, 2007. The GOZ allowance could be as high as $100,000 over the usual allowance, and its phase-out limit was $600,000 larger than the limit for the regular allowance. It also affected a broader range of tangible depreciable assets as compared to the usual stipend.

The Tax Increase Prevention and Reconciliation Act of 2005 extended the changes in the allowance made by JGTRRA through 2009.

In the U.S. Troop Readiness, Veterans' Care, Katrina Recovery, and Iraq Appropriations Act, 2007, Congress decided to extend those amendments through 2010, increased the maximum allowance to $125,000, and the phase-out limits to $500,000 for tax years commencing from 2007 to 2010, and subjected both amounts to inflation in the same period. The special GOZ allowance also extended through 2008.

Congress raised the allowance to $250,000 to stimulate more investments during a severe economic meltdown. Congress also raised the phase-out threshold to $800,000 for certain assets that met specific requirements and were bought and placed in service in 2008 in the Economic Stimulus Act of 2008. The act stipulates that these amounts were supposed to reset at $125,000 and $500,000 in 2009 and 2010 respectively, and these amounts were indexed for inflation.

Several laws passed during the 111th Congress amended the Section 179 expensing allowance once again. The American Recovery and Reinvestment Act of 2009 had an effect on the Economic Stimulus Act through 2009, where it increased and improved the allowance from the Economic Stimulus Act, and the Hiring Incentives to Restore Employment Act of 2010 further extended it through 2010.

2010 Small Business Jobs Act

Under the Small Business Jobs Act of 2010, the expensing allowance increased to $500,000 and the phase-out threshold to $2 million for tax years beginning in 2010 and 2011. Starting in 2012 and after that, the maximum allowance was scheduled to reset at $25,000 and the phase-out limit at $200,000. The act also widened the meaning of qualified property to include recognized qualified restaurant property, retail improvement property, and leasehold improvement property. In 2010 and 2011, under Section 179, a business could write off to a limit of $250,000 of the annual cost of these.

The Tax Relief, Unemployment Compensation Reauthorization, and Job Creation Act of 2010 increased the maximum allowance to $125,000 and the phase-out limit to $500,000 for certified assets purchased and placed in service in 2012, subjected those sums to inflation, capped the maximum allowance at $25,000 and the phase-out limit at $200,000 commencing in 2013 and also for subsequent years. It also extended the suitability specific computer software for the allowance through 2012.

The American Taxpayer Tax Relief Act of 2012 resulted in the maximum expensing allowance to hike up to $500,000 and the phase-out threshold to $2 million in 2012 and 2013. The act also purchased off-the-shelf software claimable for the allowance in 2013 capped at a sum of $250,000 expensing allowance for qualified improvement property that first became available in 2010.

In December 2014, Congress delayed through 2014 the Section 179 expensing allowance that has been in place since 2012 and 2013 through the enactment of the Tax Increase Prevention Act of 2014.

Almost a year later, Congress once again extended the $500,000 allowance and $2 million phase-out limits from 2012 and 2013. Following the Protecting Americans from Tax Hikes Act of 2015, the Section 179 expensing allowance was set in stone at $500,000 and the phase-out limits at $2 million, beginning in 2015. Both of these amounts - the expensing allowance and phase-out limits - have been subjected to inflation since 2016. Off-the-shelf computer software and retail improvement property became permanently eligible for the allowance. The cost limit on the amount of improvement property that could be expensed in a tax year was also removed.

Congress made critical amendments in Section 179 with the passage of a tax-revision bill in December 2018 which will eventually become known as the TCJA. Based on the new tax law, the maximum expensing allowance has risen to $1 million and the phase-out limit to $2.5 million, and both sums are indexed for inflation starting in 2019. Also, the TCJA widens the scope of real property that fits the requirement for the Section 179 allowance to include the subsequent improvements to nonresidential real property: air-conditioning units; ventilation; heating; roofs; alarm system; fire protection; and security systems. It also abolishes the previous exclusion of property affiliated to housing and subjected it to inflation for the $25,000 expensing limit for heavy-duty motor vehicles.

Section 168

The Job Creation and Worker Assistance Act of 2002 created the Bonus Depreciation Allowance (BDA). It was pegged to 30% of a company's adjusted basis in qualified property purchased and operationalize between September 12, 2001, and December 31, 2004. A one-year extension of that deadline was available for a property using MACRS recovery periods of 10 years and more and more extended production periods as well as for certain forms of aircraft.

Congress had decided to introduce the Jobs and Growth Tax Relief Reconciliation Act of 2003 and raised the allowance of a company's adjusted basis by half in qualified property purchased and operational on May 6, 2003, and before January 1, 2006. This delayed the dateline for properties that have more extended production periods.

The Economic Stimulus Act of 2008 revitalized the 50% BDA overdue at the end of 2005. It affected qualified property purchased and operational in 2008. Subsequently, in 2008, Congress approved the Housing Assistance Tax Act of 2008. It added a stipulation that gave C corporations the choice to switch any BDA they could claim for property purchased and operational between April 1 and December 31, 2008, for a compensable tax credit tagged to the lesser of $30 million or 6% of the total amount of any research. AMT credits were also allowed to be carried forward from tax years before 2006.

The American Recovery and Reinvestment Act of 2009 extended the 50% BDA and the elective reimbursed credit through 2009. Congress widened the qualifications of the 50% allowance and the respective credits to qualified property acquired and operational in 2010 by passing the Small Business Jobs Act of 2010.

Based on the Tax Relief, Unemployment Compensation Reauthorization, and Job Creation Act of 2010, the BDA rose to 100% for qualified property purchased and operationalized from September 9, 2010, to December 31, 2011. The act also set a 50% allowance for property purchased and operational in 2012. However, it limited the free reimbursed credit to any untouched AMT credits from tax years before 2006; unused research tax credits within the same period could not be monetized in this manner as before.

The ATRA held out to the 50% BDA through 2013. The ATRA also lengthened the reversible elective credit through 2013 for AMT credits brought forward from tax years before 2006.

The Tax Increase Prevention Act of 2014 (TIPA) lengthened the time of the 50% BDA through 2014.

In December 2015, the Protecting Americans from Tax Hikes Act of 2015 was enacted. Among many things, the BDA was held out through 2019. From 2015 to 2017, the allowance was set to half of the price of the purchased qualified property and must have been placed in service during that period. This rate was scheduled to drop to 40% in 2018, and then to 30% in 2019. No allowance will not be available in 2020 or after that. The act also extended through 2019 the refundable elective credit. The difference between this credit and that during the period from 2008 to 2015 is the fact that for the latter, there was a stipulated dollar threshold on the claimable amount while the latter is just BDA. Besides, the scope of the BDA was expanded, taking into consideration grafted trees and private plantations or vines that bore products which had a pre-production period of more than two years from seeding to harvesting.

Its bonus depreciation amount determines the claimable amount of credit that a corporation has. However, as stipulated under Section 53(b), the bonus depreciation amount has to be higher than at least half of the corporation's AMT credit, for the company's first tax year in 2016 or for other years, determined by only including the adjusted new minimum tax (as stipulated in Section 53(d)) for tax years prior to 2016.

Congress made some significant changes in the BDA. Ideally, the act fixed the rate for the BDA at 100% for qualified property purchased and operational between September 28, 2017 and December 31, 2022. This rate has been predetermined to drop to 80% for operational property in 2023; 60% in 2024; 40% in 2025; 20% in 2026; and 0% starting in 2027 onwards. Every date of operationalization is delayed by a year for long-production property and individual aircraft. Property eligible for BDA includes fruits and nuts producing livestock. As a result of ambiguity in the language used in the final bill, qualified improvement property is not eligible for BDA until Congress amends the law and attaches a 15-year recovery period to such property. Under the act, rate-regulated utilities acquired and operational on and after September 28, 2017, does not fit the criteria for the BDA. However, purchasing of qualified used property operational during the same timing does satisfy the criteria for the allowance. Similarly, such qualified used property includes live theatrical productions and television productions within the same timeline. The choice to claim a refundable AMT credit instead of a BDA is repealed for tax years starting in 2018 and after that.

Bonus Depreciation (Section 168)

Under pre-TCJA law, for latest qualified assets that a business operationalized in 2017, you can claim a 50% first-year bonus depreciation deduction. This is a tax break, and it includes assets such as machinery, types of equipment, office furniture, and computer systems, newly purchased software, vehicles, and many more. Also, this tax break applies to qualified improvement property. Used assets, however, are not eligible for the 50% first-year bonus depreciation.

As mentioned earlier, it is permissible for qualified improvement property (QIP) to claim the 50% first-year bonus depreciation. QIP is primarily determined as any justified improvement to the interior of a non-residential building. A point to note is that such improvements must have been taken place after this non-residential building has already been operationalized. The costs of these improvements do not include the expansion of the building, the construction of an escalator, elevators, or strengthening of the building's internal structural framework.

For companies who have been exploiting the 50% bonus depreciation allowance, here is a piece of good news for all of you. With the enactment of the TCJA, the percentage of claimable bonus depreciation has been increased from 50% to 100% for qualified assets and property placed in service between September 28, 2017, and December 31, 2022. However, the increment does not apply to all sorts of property. Whether a property is eligible for it depends on the time that it was operational. Under the TCJA, the bonus depreciation percentage applies only for qualified assets and property purchased after September 28, 2017, and operational after January 1, 2018. Anything else before these dates is eligible for the 50% rates, however, provided that all other criteria have been fulfilled. This bonus depreciation percentage phases starts in 2023, decreasing by 20% annually, and finally entirely phased-out by the end of 2026. Of course, this is subjected to Congress's decision to extend the tax break.

For a specific property with extended production periods, any other reductions are delayed for a period of one year. Let us take an example to highlight this case. For properties that are meant for long production periods that will be in serviceable condition in 2024 instead of 2023.

Under the proposed provision, "qualified property" for bonus depreciation purposed will include:

- Any Quality Improvement Property (QIP) purchased after September 27, 2017 and operational, before January 1, 2018, is eligible for a 100% first-year bonus depreciation as well

- Specified Plants

- Qualified live theatrical productions, and

- Qualified film or television productions

- Water utility property

- Certain computer software

- Property depreciated using MACRS and has a 20 year recovery period.

Congress had initially wanted to include QIPs that were operationalized after 2017 to have a 15-year MACRS recovery period, which would have qualified QIPs for the bonus. However, due to some administrative oversight, the 15-year recovery period for QIP was not highlighted in any provisions of the TCJA. As a result, since QIPs operationalized after 2017 has a 39-year MACRS recovery period, such QIPs are, therefore, ineligible for bonus depreciation.

The proposed provisions also detail how taxpayers can elect out of bonus depreciation. These provisions have laid out the requirements as to how taxpayers can opt for the 50% bonus depreciation rather than the 100% bonus depreciation. This flexibility, however, is only available for properties purchased after September 27, 2017, and put into operation within that taxable year.

Special rules apply for more extended production period property and individual aircraft. The criteria for properties eligible for the 100% bonus depreciation was expanded to include used qualified properties purchased and operational after September 27, 2017, if all the following factors apply:

If a property becomes accepted for bonus depreciation, then the cost of that particular property excludes any costs affiliated to any additional properties or third-parties (for example, in a like-kind exchange or involuntary conversion).

The taxpayers already have full authority over the used property and can't be a case where the authority of the property is still pending, such as from a decedent.

The taxpayer has full authority over the used property purchased without any affiliation or reference to the seller, or a decedent.

The taxpayer did not purchase the property from a component member of a controlled group of corporations.

The taxpayer did not purchase the property from a related party.

The taxpayer or its predecessor did not use the property at any time before acquiring it.

Business tenants can claim the bonus depreciation provided that the lease of the lessee has ended. Assuming that the property also falls under QIPs, the amount of bonus depreciation that the property is eligible for excludes the cost of the improvements made to the property.

For acquisition of depreciable interests, only the primary one is eligible for the bonus depreciation. Subsequent acquisitions of depreciable interests will not have the same qualities as compared to the previous depreciable interest, unless the new depreciable interest replaces the preceding depreciable interest, then the new depreciable interest will have the same qualities as the previous depreciable interest in that property, capped at the amount of the portion for which the business held a depreciable interest in that property.

The used property also must satisfy certain related party and carryover basis requirements, as well as certain cost requirements. This includes anti-abuse provisions for members of a consolidated group, certain acquisitions following a series of related transactions, and syndication transactions. They also explained how the new bonus depreciation rules apply to a variety of transactions involving partnerships holdings; assets that qualify for the bonus depreciation as well such as vehicles or used machinery.

Date of Acquisition

The TCJA states that property will not be treated as acquired by the opening party the moment a "written binding contract" is signed with the acquirer with regard to the acquisition. The TCJA clarifies that any other dates including cash delivery dates or closing dates do not play a role at all. The TCJA emphasizes that once the contract is signed, the property will no longer be considered as 'acquired' by the initial owner of that property.

Under the TCJA, a written contract is legally binding the moment it is within the jurisdiction of state law against a taxpayer, and there are no limits, whatsoever, to the number of damages. Even if there is a clause specifying the damages in case of a breach in contract, as long as it remains lower than 5% of the total contractual value, this clause will not be considered as limiting damages. Hence, such a contract will still be legally binding under the eyes of the law.

A letter stating the intent of a buyer to acquire another company cannot be a substitute or a proxy for a binding contract. Further, a supply agreement is not treated as written binding contracts until a taxpayer provides the value and design blueprints of the property. The TCJA eliminates the protection clause for self-constructed properties. Initially, even after a written-binding contract has been signed, a self-constructed property is still considered as such and falls under the authority of the initial owner. The removal of this protection means that such properties will lose its status as a self-constructed property the moment the acquisition contract is signed.

Actual self-constructed property is not subjected to the written binding contract requirement. The new acquisition rules mentioned above apply to all self-constructed properties from the moment a taxpayer begins manufacturing, constructing, or producing the property from September 27, 2017, onwards.

Companies dealing with matters with regard to mergers, acquisitions, and divestitures should take particular notice to this section because of the many stipulations affecting the criteria that a used property must have before they are eligible for a depreciation bonus. Companies should also review past transactions so as to be sure that none of these transactions have contravened any existing laws, so as not to get called up by the IRS. One way in which companies can take advantage of these new stipulations during acquisition is to opt for asset purchase rather than solely stocks. This then allows companies to benefit from the bonus depreciation.

According to the TCJA, the total sum of the first-year depreciation deduction is similar to the respective percentage of that property's unadjusted depreciable amount. The unadjusted depreciable amount is usually capped to the property's primary function such as production, construction or manufacturing, before January

1, 2027.

There are also some exceptions whereby a business will not be able to claim the bonus depreciation from 2018 onwards. Such businesses include dealerships with floor-plan financing and that their average yearly gross receipts have exceeded $25 million for the past three years, and real estate businesses whereby the employees have elected to subtract 100% of their business interest.

There are multiple options for bonus depreciation available for businesses. However, not all are advantageous to all sorts of business. Some may be better in some cases while others apply better to different cases. Therefore, a business has to spend more time to analyze the different bonus depreciation, and how these will help them in their businesses.

Section 179

Section 179 gives firms of various business industries and sizes the rights to expense the cost of new and used qualified property in the tax year when these assets are placed in service. However, these are placed with certain limits. A business taxpayer that cannot claim or choose not to claim the allowance may recover capital costs over extended timelines and at reduced rates by adopting the Modified Accelerated Cost Recovery System (MACRS) or Alternative Depreciation System (ADS).

There are two important things to take note when using the Section 179 allowance. The first is called 'an investment limitation.' Under this limitation, companies should try to keep the average cost of the purchased qualified property that they have operationalized at or below the phase-out threshold determined in Section 179. This is because any amount above the threshold limit would result in a dollar for dollar reduction in the amount of allowance that a taxpayer is eligible for. From 2018 onwards, this threshold level is set at $2,500,000. What this means is that a company will not be able to claim any expensing allowance from 2018 onwards if the average cost of the purchased property is evaluated at or more than $3,500,000.

The second thing to take note of is called an 'income limitation.' The income limitations stop individuals from getting an allowance whose amount is more than his or her taxable business income before the deduction of wages.

Here's an example. Assuming a company has a taxable income of $50,000 in 2018 from its main operations, the company is then eligible to file a claim under Section 179 for an allowance of $75,000 under the investment limitation. However, the company can only expense up to $50,000 of the initial cost of that property and fill the remaining $25,000 through applying the MACRS or carry this amount of $25,000 to any subsequent tax year when the Company can subtract this amount under Section 179.

Due to the investment limitation, individuals will not be permitted to bring forward any remaining allowances from the actual tax year. However, they can bring forward any amount of allowances if these allowances have been left over due to income limitation.

Before claiming the allowance, an individual has to fill in Form 4562, including the items that the election applies and the amount of each item that is to be subtracted. Ideally, the election can only be revoked with the consent of the IRS. However, Congress has repealed this stipulation since 2002. This means that individuals may now choose to nullify any part of the election to expense qualified property without the need to seek the authority of the IRS. The amendment holds regardless of whether the elections were made on an original return or not. To nullify the election, the individual needs to resubmit his or her return for the tax year, and adopt an alternative depreciation method.

In circumstances whereby one fails to meet the criteria for a 100% first-year bonus depreciation, the expense allowance stipulated in Section 179 will be able to cover such circumstances. Section 179 permits individuals who fit the criteria to deduct the full cost of qualified new or old depreciable property, including most software and QIPs in year 1. Of course, there is no free lunch in this world, and one can expect that there are bound to be certain caveats to Section 179 as well.

Under pre-TCJC law, for tax years that began in 2017, the maximum Section 179 depreciation deduction was capped at $510,000. The ceiling deduction is phased out dollar-for-dollar when the average cost of the operational property increased beyond the limit that was capped at $2.03 million. This means that if you owned a property that is worth $500,000 more than the threshold value of $2.53 million, you would only receive $10,000 depreciation deduction.

The TCJA permanently enhances the depreciation that will be deducted as part of the Section 179. Under the new law, certain properties operational from 2018 onwards, will have the maximum deduction risen to $1 million. However, the phase-out limit has been raised to a level of $2.5 million. These amounts will be adjusted for inflation as time goes by.

This means that if you have a property that is worth $500,000 more than the threshold value of $2.5 million, you will still be eligible for a depreciation deduction of $1 million as compared to the previous deduction of $10,000.

The TCJA has widened its scope of the eligible property. From 2018 onwards, certain tangible personal property that is used to improve the decor of the property and is depreciable qualifies for the Section 179 deduction. Such examples of tangible personal property include simple things like alarm and security systems to more complex items like HVAC equipment.

Depreciation of Luxury Automobiles and Personal Property

The Section 179 deduction has always been one of the critical favorites for businesses who possess vehicles. Before the TCJA, the Section 179 deduction allowed businesses to abuse the provision and write off the cost of large SUVs, regardless of the type and frequency of usage of it, and thereby earning the notorious nickname - 'Hummer Tax Loophole.'

With the TCJA, businesses will not be able to exploit the Section 179 deductions as they did before. This is due to the several limitations imposed under the TCJA with regard to claiming deductions for vehicles. Nonetheless, it is still advantageous for businesses to tap into the benefits of Section 179 when it comes to purchasing vehicles for business usage.

Under the amendments, businesses wanting to claim full deductions for purchased vehicles under Section 179, can only do so for vehicles that are being used solely for business purposes. It is the responsibility of the company to prove that the purchased vehicle is indeed business related. Nevertheless, some passenger vehicles are still eligible for some form of deduction which is capped at $11,160.

It is arguable that many vehicles serve dual purposes - both business related and for personal reasons. As such, the stipulations with regard to business vehicle deductions are not set in stone. Instead, they need to evolve with time making it complicated. For now, it would be neater just to note down the vehicles that will be eligible for a full Section 179 deduction, before proceeding to talk about the deductions - if any - for other function vehicles.

One can be assured that vehicles that are solely used for business purposes will qualify for full Section 179 deduction. So what will constitute a business vehicle?

Typical "over-the-road" Tractor Trailers will qualify.

Heavy construction equipment will qualify for the Section 179 deduction, similar for forklifts.

Vehicles with: (1) a fully-enclosed driver's compartment or cargo area, (2) no seating at all behind the driver's seat, and (3) no parts of the vehicle should be protruding more than 30 inches ahead of the windshield. It should just look like any typical cargo van.

Vehicles that can seat nice-plus passengers behind the driver's seat (i.e., Hotel / Airport shuttle vans, etc.)

Typical Passenger Vehicles used for Business

It is understandable that at times, passenger vehicles have to double up for business usages. Unfortunately, such vehicles are not allowed to have the full Section 179 expense deduction.

For passenger vehicles, trucks, and vans (not meeting the guidelines below) that are used in more than 50% of actual business requirements, the total deduction that is allowed for both the Section 179 expense deduction and Bonus Depreciation is capped at $11,160 for cars and $11,560 for trucks and large vehicles such as vans. Exceptions include the following vehicles:

Heavy "non-SUV" vehicles or trucks with a cargo area and a interior length of minimally six feet (this area must not be easily accessible from the passenger area). For example, many trucks are modified with cargo beds, and these trucks will be eligible for the full sum of Section 179 deduction.

Qualified nonpersonal use vehicles specially modified for business (e.g., work van without seating behind the driver, constructing of shelves within the vehicles, and those having stickers on exterior showing the company's name).

Vehicles used to transport people such as taxis or property for hire individually.

Ambulance or hearses explicitly used for business purposes.

Newly imposed limitations for SUVs or Crossover Vehicles with GVW above 6,000lbs.

Remember that I previously mentioned about businesses abusing the Section 179 deduction before the TCJA and simply writing off the cost of SUVs, regardless of what the use of it is for? With the TCJA, there have been several impositions that will help in reducing such abuses. For SUVs and other larger vehicles to qualify for the full sum of the deduction, these vehicles must be a 4-wheeled vehicle that is mainly used to transport passengers over public roads. These vehicles must also be between 6,000 lbs. to 14,000 lbs. gross vehicle weight.

The TCJA has also amended the ceiling of depreciation that passenger vehicles operational from 2018 onwards can claim. Assuming that the individual chooses not to claim bonus depreciation, the most substantial amount of deduction that the individual can claim will be as follows:

- $10,000 for the first year

- $16,000 for the second year

- $9,600 for the third year

- $5,760 for each subsequent year in the recovery period.

However, should the taxpayer opt for a 100% bonus depreciation, the allowable depreciation deduction is as follows:

- $18,000 for the first year

- $16,000 for the second year

- $9,600 for the third year, and

- $5,760 for each subsequent year in the recovery period.

Whether a vehicle is new or used does not matter as long as it is new to you. In other words, the vehicle must have been recently purchased by you in a short transaction under the company's name and covered with proper financial loans. The vehicle must also be used primarily for business functions for more than half the time. The corresponding percentage of personal use reduces these depreciation limits if the vehicle is used for business less than 100% of the time. For example, a passenger vehicle, which cost $25,000, was purchased and put into use during 2018 and forward through 2022. This vehicle was used 75% of the time for business purposes, so your basis for Section 179 calculation is $18,750. This is $8,750 more than the first-year limit, and therefore, only $10,000 can be deducted.

The TCJA also removes the computer or peripheral equipment from the definition of listed property. From 2018 onwards, the value of deductions will be indexed for inflation. One might argue that the pre-TCJA law is more beneficial for business because it allows the maximum amount to have been a deduction in year 1, thus allowing businesses to report a lower income and hence lower taxable income. However, it is also important to note that the TCJA does allow for a faster depreciation and hence achieving the same effect as the pre-TCJA law.

For example, under pre-TCJA law, the 2017 deduction for a passenger car is capped at $11,160 for Year 1 provided that the car is new and that bonus depreciation is included (note that it is $3,160 for a used car). For subsequent years, the limits for both new and used cars, are $5,100, $3,050, and $1,875 respectively. Just for your information, slightly higher caps are applied to light trucks and light vans. So, one can easily make a comparison and realize that the amendments under the TCJA are much more favorable towards business vehicles.

In general, a company possessing assets that fit the criteria for both Section 179 and Section 168 expensing allowances has to conduct its claims in a prescribed order. The company has to file a claim under Section 179 to lower the company's stake in that asset by the filed amount. Next, the company can apply for the bonus depreciation allowance to the remaining value of the asset. Finally, the company will then claim a depreciation allowance either under the MACRS, adopting a double declining balance method for the remaining value of the asset.

Let us take a look at a simple illustration of the process. Company A has purchased 10 new machine tools at a total cost of $1 million. This would, automatically, qualify the company for the Section 179 expensing allowance of $500,000, and, therefore, bring the value of the tools to $500,000. The tools will also qualify for the bonus depreciation allowance, and hence a further 50% of the acquisition cost would be subtracted. Once this step has been completed, the company can then opt to recover the remaining cost under the MACRS method on the remaining $250,000. Since the MACRS recovery period for machine tools is five years, and that five-year property will depreciate based on the double-declining-balance method, the company will accept an additional depreciation allowance, which is equivalent to 20% of $250,000, or $50,000. The MACRS depreciation deduction will then settle the remaining $200,000 over the next five years at 32%, 19.2%, 11.52%, and 5.76% respectively.

As a result, the company will technically save up to 89% of the cost of the machine tools that it bought.

Applicable Recovery Period for Real Property

When depreciation is involved, then it has recovery periods. The recovery periods for non-residential real property and residential rental property are pegged at 39 years and 27.5 years respectively. The recovery rule established for the recovery of the non-residential real property does not include changes and still remains at 40 years. However, the TCJA has reduced the recovery period for residential rental property from 40 to 30 years. Leasehold improvement properties, restaurant properties, and retail improvement properties that meet the criteria will be lumped together as a single entity and will no longer have a 15-year recovery period. These amendments under the TCJA will only affect properties operational from 2018 onwards. Besides, any real estate business that opts out of the business interest deduction limit will be obliged to adopt the alternative depreciation system for its non-residential real properties, residential rental properties, and qualified improvements properties. All these amendments kicked in starting 2018.

Chapter **13**

Business Credits

Rehabilitation Tax Credit

The rehabilitation tax credit is a federal tax incentive to encourage real estate developers to renovate, restore, and reconstruct old buildings. Buildings placed in service before 1936 can claim a 10% credit and 20% credit for qualified historic structures. The credit solely applies to the occupancy costs, and not the cost of the building or cost incurred to beautify its surroundings. Interestingly, the amount of credit eligible for such structures is higher if the structure is situated in a specific declared disaster area. The program has been one of the nation's most successful community revitalization programs, encouraging private sector investment, creating jobs, and preserving our architectural heritage for generations.

With the implementation of the TCJA, the rules surrounding the tax credits have changed. From 2018 onwards, individuals are eligible to 20% credit over five years instead of claiming the full sum within the year that the building was re-operationalized. The TCJA also eliminates the 10% rehabilitation credit for pre-1936 buildings. This provision is sufficient for payments made from 2018 onwards.

Nevertheless, there is a transition rule that helps to ease the financial toll on owners of a pre-1936 building or a qualified historic structure. This transition rule allows owners to activate the pre-TCJA law instead of the present one, provided that their projects fulfill two conditions:

- The 24- or 60-month period chosen for the re-occupation test commence by June 20, 2018.

- The taxpayer owns or leases the building inclusively on January 1, 2018, and continues to do so.

So, what impact do these amendments have? First, the 20% tax credit functions like free equity: a developer can use it to offset its federal corporate tax liability or, more often, can sell the credits to investors to generate capital for equity. The most impactful change of the bill is the ability for individuals to claim the credit throughout five years as compared to claiming all at once within the year that the project has materialized. What is the big deal you ask? Well, the difference is that of inflation. A 5-year stretch reduces the credit's value by almost 20%. Thus, this change in the rehabilitation tax credit can leave a big gap in project financing, rendering a once-feasible project infeasible. Such a conclusion could result in developers choosing to demolish these historic structures rather than rehabilitating it.

Employer Credit for Paid Family and Medical Leave

The Family and Medical Leave Act (FMLA) of 1993 dictates that all covered employers are to allow their employees to go on leave for family and medical matters of up to 12 work weeks annually. However, no segment of the act states that employees are eligible for compensation during their period of absence. The TCJA throws in a new provision that allows employers to claim tax credits whenever their employee goes on such an absence. The number of tax credits will be correlated to the salary of the individual employee that is on leave, subject to certain conditions.

This new employer credit will only apply from the beginning of 2018 to the end of 2019. To claim this compensation credit, the amount of disbursed compensation for each employee during the previous year must not be above a certain amount, which varies from year to year. For example, for the tax year of 2018, the employee's 2017 compensation from the employers must have been $72,000 or less.

The amount of salary that the employer can claim under the compensation credit is determined by the Federal Unemployment Tax Act (FUTA). However, it disregards the FUTA wage threshold of $7,000. The compensation credit tends only to be a portion of the total sum of wages paid to employees during their time off - for medical and family matters. Alternatively, staff employees can also apply for a Leave of Absence (LOA) for similar matters which is covered under Title I of the Family and Medical Leave Act of 1993.

More importantly, employers must have a written policy in place that meets specific requirements. Some of these requirements include:

The written policy must include the employer's continued commitment to disburse at least half of the employee's wages while the latter is on leave.

The written policy needs to explicitly state that all full-time employees are given the right to go for a minimum of two weeks of annual time off to settle family and medical matters . Even for part-time workers, the policy needs to include the pro-rated number of days that they can go on time off for similar matters.

This only applies to employees who have worked at that company for a year or longer and received a compensation amount the preceding year which surmounted to less than a certain threshold level, usually capped at $72,000.

The written policy has to be a blanket policy, encompassing all the employees in the company.

In the case that there happen to be staff members who are not covered under Title I of the FMLA, the company's written policy must explicitly state the "non-interference" protections for these staff members, as illustrated in Section A of Note 2018-71. Hence, the written policy must include, if possible, all the regulations and criteria for the employer to claim the compensation credits.

For employees under government service or receiving wages from government-related organizations, do note that these wages will not be considered for the credit. In other words, the employer is not eligible to apply for the compensation credit.

Length-of-service awards for public safety volunteers

Length-of-service awards are issued as a form of gratitude by employers to their employees for working for them over a sustained period. Usually, to qualify for a length-of-service award, the minimum duration is about five years.

There are different regulations stipulated under Section 457, governing delayed compensations disbursed by state and local government, and private, tax-exempted employers. As for every stipulation, exceptions happen. In this case, compensation disbursed to genuine volunteers as part of their length-of-service award is one such exception and is governed by different regulations. Note that these volunteers have to be doing work with regard to governing public safety, such as ambulance service, emergency medical services, firefighting, and fire prevention services. An individual must fulfill this criterion to be seen as a bona fide public safety volunteer. Also, because these volunteers are technically not workers or employees, they are not eligible for full-time wages. However, these volunteers do, at times, receive some form of recognition by their employers such as cash or awards. However, for an individual to sustain his status as a volunteer, the amount of compensation that the volunteer receives for his volunteering services must be a 'reasonable' amount which is usually based on the market rate. If they are not reimbursed in terms of cash, then these volunteers should at least receive some form of 'reasonable' benefits to recognize their volunteering efforts such as length-of-service awards. However, the deviation from Section 457 in governing these volunteers will only be applicable if the average length-of-service awards given to a volunteer within a year is below $3,000.

Amendments under the TCJA

From 2018 onwards, the previously agreed threshold level of $3,000 will be increased to $6,000 and is set to increase by $500 every year to reflect inflations in the cost of living. If the agreement between the employer and the volunteer is a detailed plan encompassing the benefits, similar to that of a contract, then the $6,000 limit will only apply to the present value of the average amount of length-of-service awards within a year. While the present value of any future disbursements can only be calculated based on certain assumptions, these assumptions have to be reasonable and only specific methods can be used. One of the critical assumptions is that these disbursements will be paid in cash following the earliest period that these benefits have to be disbursed or the age of the volunteer.

Companies that are governed by Section 457 and have public safety volunteers under their charge should review their existing policies. Given the increment of the threshold level for the number of disbursements that a volunteer can receive, companies have to think about whether an increased length-of-service of these volunteers would be beneficial for them or not. If not, then perhaps companies should start to reduce their reliance on such volunteers.

Chapter **14**

Business Related Losses

Net Operating Loss Deduction (NOL)

Companies and businesses may have to adjust their existing tax filing strategies especially when it comes to net operating losses deductions. Net Operating Losses (NOL) can occur in any year as long as the companies' deductions surpass its operating income, resulting in a negative operating income and hence constituting a loss. Before the TCJA, companies tend to either "carryback" or "carryforward" their taxes whereby companies apply for NOL tax deductions on their former tax returns either two years back or two years ahead.

The TCJA has removed the privilege of business owners in executing a "carryback." From 2018 onwards, companies are only allowed to carry forward NOLs. Instead of just limited to two years, companies will now be able to carry forward to an unlimited number of years. However, unlike the pre-TCJA era where 100% of a company's taxable income can be deduced from NOLs, the TCJA amended the percentage permissible, limiting it to 80%.

There are also new limitations with regard to deducting

"excess business losses." The number of deductible business losses for companies are capped at $250,000 per individual or $500,000 for married couples that are filing a joint return. Any residual amount after the deduction must be brought forward to the next year. This new stipulation will apply to all businesses less C corporations from 2018 onwards until the end of 2025.

Roth IRA conversion and NOL deduction

A tip for companies: understand that there is a difference between NOLs and net capital losses. For the latter, the maximum amount that can be used to subtract from an ordinary income is capped at $3,000. However, since there are fewer regulations on the usage of NOL in subtracting from ordinary incomes, companies should exploit this benefit. For example, individuals who have opted to carry forward NOLs can use these losses to reduce the amount of taxable income incurred during a Roth IRA conversion. Let us take a look at a simple illustration.

Tom owns a company and within the year of 2018, incurred an NOL of $200,000 after listing down the various business income and losses on Schedule C. Tom also has to his name a SEP-IRA account containing $500,000. Tom and his spouse have an accumulated taxable income of $100,000 from earnings and income from other investment accounts. Since the NOL incurred in 2018, Tom and his spouse can only carry forward their NOL deductions and are only allowed to subtract up to 80% of their total taxable income.

If they did not execute an IRA conversion, the amount of taxable income left after an NOL deduction of $80,000 would be $20,000 with the remaining amount of NOL to be brought forward to subsequent years. However, if Tom had opted to swap from a SEP-IRA account to a Roth IRA account and transferred $150,000 from the former to the latter, Tom and his spouse will be able to delete the entire $200,000 worth of NOL and end up reporting only $50,000 of taxable income. Now, some of you may be questioning the logic of this move since they will not be reporting a higher amount of taxable income than before. However, while this is the case, for the first scenario, they would have converted $150,000 in pretax SEP-IRA assets to a tax-free IRA while avoiding a carry forward of the NOL.

Limitation on Losses Other than Corporations

Before the TCJA, individual taxpayers could deduct business losses without a limit on the amount. They could then deduct these losses in the current year.

From the beginning of the tax years ending after December 31, 2017, and before January 1, 2026, the TCJA limits business losses for non-corporate individuals. An individual will be eligible for deductions for business losses based on the number of gains, with an additional $250,000 thrown in, in the same year. For joint returns, the additional bonus will be $500,000. Both of these bonuses will be indexed for inflation. Assuming that the business loss surpasses that limit, this would create excess business losses, and thereby label as an NOL and carried forward to the next years. Partnerships and S corporations apply these rules at the partner or shareholder level.

The calculation of an individual's business loss can only be done so after the application of the passive loss rules. Any additional business losses, once these losses exceed the gain within the same year, can only be treated as an NOL and brought forward to subsequent years. For example, John and his spouse have a combined taxable income of $1 million and have incurred a net loss of $2 million including $500,000 of passive losses and $1.5 million from active business operations, in the year of 2018. Based on these figures, subtracting the gains from the business from the operating losses will give you the number of net business losses which is $1 million. This $1 million will then be carried forward to subsequent years as an NOL.

Since John and his spouse will be filing a joint return, they will have a business deduction bonus of $500,000. Hence, their Adjusted Gross Income (AGI) will come to the amount to $500,000.

Before the enactment of the TCJA, the taxpayer would have had the passive loss carried forward which is valued at $500,000. However, carrying forward of their passive loss would result in their adjusted gross income to be at negative $500,000 ($1,000,000 of wages less $1,500,000 of non-passive and passive losses). This means that John and his spouse will not be liable for taxes.

The treasury has been tasked to oversee such issues, and hence it will implement specific additional requirements to ensure that all loopholes of this provision will be appropriately covered.

Chapter **15**

Miscellaneous Provisions

Opportunity Zones

Opportunity Zones are economic development tools created to encourage tax-favored investments in afflicting communities throughout the country and U.S. owned territories. The recently enacted provision (Section 1400Z-2) provides advantages for investments in these zones only if the investments come from a fund known as the Qualified Opportunity Fund (QOF) within a corporation. To set up funds, a company must either be a partnership or that they intend to invest in pre-determined qualified properties situated within the Qualified Opportunity Zones.

Once returns are realized in these investments in these Opportunity Zones, there will be unique tax benefits for either the partnership or the corporation. These benefits include:

A delay in the taxation of the returns in investment assets made within the Opportunity Zones using funds from the QOF until the appreciated asset is sold in the market or by December 31, 2026, whichever comes first.

A 10% exclusion of the deferred gain after five years, which grows to 15% after seven years. If the investor held the appreciated asset for more than 10 years, then the returns made from the asset, even if it was sold, will not be liable for taxation.

A corporation or partnership that sets up as QOF has to continue to meet specific requirements unless they wished to be awarded certain penalties. The corporation or partnership must adhere to recordkeeping requirements based on the IRS, and it is the responsibility of the corporation or the partnership to be able to prove their QOF status during the audit and hence the right to delay taxation on the returns made through the investments. Investors are also required to adhere to recordkeeping requirements just for tracking purposes.

S Corporations

The TCJA has widened the criteria of personnel who can take on the role as inheritors of Electing Small Business Trusts (ESBTs). Previously, non-resident aliens were not permitted as S corporation shareholders. However, effective January 1, 2018, non-resident aliens can become inheritors of ESBTs. Non-resident aliens can be defined as individuals who are non-U.S. citizens, yet neither are they permanent residents residing in the U.S.

Conversion from S to C

As you may have now known, the tax rates for C corporations are set at a flat rate of 21%. So, what about S corporations? For one, S corporations can convert to C corporations to enjoy the same benefits. However, the TCJA has added two new requirements for this conversion to be approved. First, the S corporation has to abandon its 'S' status by withdrawing from its election between December 21, 2017, and December 22, 2019. Second, the stock owners of S corporations' stocks must be the same people and the same proportions, up until the date that the S corporation abandons its status.

Several amendments apply to S corporations

The duration for adding net adjustments due to the conversion of the S corporation election has been lengthened to six years. The need to include these net adjustments could be a result of a switch in accounting methods from cash to accrual which is a requirement if the S corporation wishes to convert to a C corporation. The six-year duration will only apply to net adjustments that either increases or lowers a corporation's taxable income. Any subsequent payouts of cash, once the S-corporation has successfully converted to C-corporation, will be seen as part of the corporation's accumulated adjustments account containing the earnings and profits proportionally.

Farm Provisions

There are two main provisions concerning the farming business.

First, the TCJA has reduced the depreciable recovery period for newly operationalized farming machinery and equipment from 2018 onwards. Initially, the depreciable duration was seven years, but it is now five years instead. However, specific equipment such as grain bins, cotton ginning assets, fences, and other land improvements, which may be related to farming are not subjected to this amended depreciable recovery duration.

Second, farming businesses who choose to opt out of the interest deduction limit will only be allowed to use the alternative depreciation system for any property which has a depreciation recovery period of 10 years and above. Such property includes agricultural or horticultural structures, trees or vines bearing fruit or nuts, farm buildings, and certain land improvements. This provision will take effect from 2018 onwards. Properties used in a farming business and operational from 2018 onwards will no longer be forced to adopt the 150% declining balance method. However, if the property is a 15-year or 20-year property, the taxpayer must continue to use the 150% declining balance method.

Conclusion

All in all, it appears that the TCJA is largely centered on businesses and that of the family especially with the expansion of family credits and also the creation of the other dependent credits. It is little wonder that most large corporations have applauded the TCJA as the tax benefits have helped to save billions of dollars that would have, otherwise, been paid to the IRS.

I cannot emphasize how important it is for anyone to internalize this book. As I have illustrated throughout, the TCJA has resulted in tremendous changes to previous tax laws. However, there is no need to be afraid because I have done most of the job for you by summarizing the key parts of the amendments that may probably affect you and your loved ones. For individuals, the key thing to take note of is the suspension of personal exemptions and the amendments made to the itemizing of items. Especially for people who have been relying on these tax breaks for previous tax years, do make sure to review your filings to make sure that you do not end up paying penalties unnecessarily. For businesses, the key changes to take note of includes the flat corporate tax of 21% which will definitely benefit the majority of businesses. Another key change to take note of is the regulation governing the usage of SUVs that weigh more than 6000lbs and the corresponding tax breaks.

I would like to reiterate that it is impossible for one to avoid paying taxes as it will simply result in unnecessary trouble. In addition, all these taxes are important to ensure the functionality of the government and the country, such as the construction of public schools, infrastructure, and other amenities. Hence, the way to approach taxation is to pay our fair share, nothing more and nothing less. The only way to do so is to ensure that we optimize the tax breaks given to us and also to take note of those changes that could be costly to us. This book will serve as a handy guide for anyone who needs to understand the changes with the implementation of the TCJA, at least all the way through 2025. I hope that you have gain lots of perspectives pertaining to the TCJA and that you have enjoyed the book.

Bibliography

Antebi, G., Krauthamer, N., & Karaman, A. F. (2018, November 12). United States: Qualified Business Income - Are you Eligible For a 20% Deduction? Part II: Additional Guidance. Retrieved from Mondaq: http://www.mondaq.com/unitedstates/x/753286/Income+Tax/Qualified+Business+Income+Are+You+Eligible+For+A+20+Deduction+Part+II+Additional+Guidance

Bryan, B. (2017, December 2). Republicans Rejoice After Senate Passes Tax Bill in Major Win for Trump, GOP. Retrieved from Business Insider: http://www.businessinsider.sg/trump-tax-reform-passed-senate-vote-count-2017-12/?r=US&IR=T

Carlson, B. (2018, September 29). What You Need To Know About The New Alternative Minimum Tax. Retrieved from Forbes: https://www.forbes.com/sites/bobcarlson/2018/09/29/what-you-need-to-know-about-the-new-alternative-minimum-tax/#74b490554822

Chandra, S. (2017, December 20). What you Need to Know About 'Chained CPI'. Retrieved from Bloomberg: https://www.bloomberg.com/news/articles/2017-11-20/why-chained-cpi-has-links-to-u-s-tax-debate-quicktake-q-a

Congressional Budget Office. (2017, November). Repealing the Individual Health Insurance Mandate: An Updated Estimate. Retrieved from Congressional Budget Office: https://www.cbo.gov/system/files?file=115th-congress-

2017-2018/reports/53300-individualmandate.pdf

Cornell Law School. (2019, February 28). 26 U.S. Code S132 Certain Fringe Benefits. Retrieved from Cornell Law: http://www.law.cornell.edu/uscode/text/26/132

Department of the Treasury Internal Revenue Service. (2019, February 28). (Circular E), Employer's Tax Guide. Retrieved from IRS: https://www.irs.gov/pub/irs-pdf/p15.pdf

Epperson, S., & Dickler, J. (2018, December 23). How to make the most of your year-end giving. Retrieved from CNBC: https://www.cnbc.com/2018/12/18/how-to-make-the-most-of-your-charitable-donations.html

Guenther, G. (2018, May 1). The Section 179 and Section 168(k): Expensing Allowances - Current Law and Economic Effects. Retrieved from Congressional Research Service: http://fas.org/sgp/crs/misc/RL31852.pdf

Internal Revenue Service. (2019, February 28). Tax Tutorial, Module 4: Dependents. Retrieved from IRS: https://apps.irs.gov/app/understandingTaxes/hows/tax_tu torials/mod04/tt_mod04_01.jsp.

IRS. (2018, May 9). Determining Alien Tax Status. Retrieved from IRS: https://www.irs.gov/individuals/international-taxpayers/determining-alien-tax-status

IRS. (2018, July 13). Like-Kind Exchanges - Real Estate Tax Tips. Retrieved from IRS: https://www.irs.gov/businesses/small-businesses-self-employed/like-kind-exchanges-real-estate-tax-tips

IRS. (2018, November 19). Like-kind exchanges now limited to real property. Retrieved from IRS:

https://www.irs.gov/newsroom/like-kind-exchanges-now-limited-to-real-property

IRS. (2018, November 5). Rehabilitation Tax Credit - Real Estate Tax Tips. Retrieved from IRS: https://www.irs.gov/businesses/small-businesses-self-employed/rehabilitation-tax-credit-real-estate-tax-tips

IRS. (2019, February 27). About Notice 1036: Early Release Copies of the Percentage Method Tables for Income Tax Withholding. Retrieved from IRS: https://www.irs.gov/forms-pubs/about-notice-1036

IRS. (2019, February 27). Adjusted Gross Income. Retrieved from IRS: https://www.irs.gov/e-file-providers/definition-of-adjusted-gross-income

Mahaffey, E. M., & Wallace, J. A. (2018, November 5). The Tax Cut and Jobs Act (the TCJA) is one of the most significant pieces of tax reform in the last 30 years. Retrieved from TIDWELL group: https://tidwellgroup.com/wp-content/uploads/2018/11/The-Tax-Cut-and-Jobs-Act-w-example.pdf

Mercado, D. (2018, October 29). Time is running out to use these 2018 tax savings tips. Retrieved from CNBC: https://www.cnbc.com/2018/10/29/time-is-running-out-to-use-these-2018-tax-savings-tips.html

Mercado, D. (2018, July 27). Why entrepreneurs should slow down before taking this tax break. Retrieved from CNBC: https://www.cnbc.com/2018/07/27/why-entrepreneurs-should-slow-down-before-taking-this-tax-break.html

Mercado, D. (2019, January 9). Here are your new income tax brackets for 2018. Retrieved from CNBC:

https://www.cnbc.com/2018/11/16/here-are-your-new-income-tax-brackets-for-2019.html

Murray, J. (2018, November 13). Pass Through Taxes and Business Owners. Retrieved from The Balance Small Business: https://www.thebalancesmb.com/pass-through-taxes-and-business-owners-398390

Nitti, T. (2018, August 9). IRS Provides Guidance on 20% Pass Through Deduction, But Questions Remains. Retrieved from Forbes: https://www.forbes.com/sites/anthonynitti/2018/08/09/irs-provides-guidance-on-20-pass-through-deduction-but-questions-remain/#27a96a172ff8

Polk, D. (2018, January 8). New Tax Act Provides Tax Deferral Opportunity for Private Company Equity Compensation Awards. Retrieved from Client Memorandum: https://www.davispolk.com/files/2018-01-08_tax_act_provides_deferral_opportunity_private_company_equity_compensation_awards.pdf

PWC. (2018, March). Tax reform changes related to meal and entertainment expenditures. Retrieved from PWC: https://www.pwc.com/us/en/services/tax/library/insights/tax-reform-changes-related-to-meal-and-entertainment-expenditure.html

RS. (2019, February 26). Topic Nmber 553: Tax on a Child's Investment and Other Unearned Income (Kiddie Tax). Retrieved from IRS: https://www.irs.gov/taxtopics/tc553

Section 179. (2018, November 5). Vehicles and Section 179. Retrieved from Section 179 Org: https://www.section179.org/section_179_vehicle_deductions/

Smith & Howard. (2018, March). 2018 Tax Cuts & Job Act Overview. Retrieved from Smith & Howard - Certified Public Accountants and Advisers: https://www.smith-howard.com/2018-tax-cuts-jobs-act-overview/

Splett, K. (2018, November 5). Changes to Tax Treatment of Qualified Transportation Fringe Benefits Under the Tax Cuts and Jobs Act. Retrieved from Wagner Tax Law: https://wagnertaxlaw.com/changes-to-tax-treatment-of-qualified-transportation-fringe-benefits-under-the-tax-cuts-and-jobs-act/

Thiel, A. (2018, February 22). Section 179 Expensing and Bonus Depreciation. Retrieved from Changes to Depreciation in the Tax Cut and Jobs Act: https://www.gordoncpa.com/2018/02/22/changes-to-depreciation-in-the-tax-cuts-and-jobs-act/